CHRISTIAN AND MUSLIM IN AFRICA

CHRISTIAN
AND MUSLIM
IN AFRICA

Noel Q. King

HARPER & ROW, PUBLISHERS
New York, Evanston, San Francisco, London
1817

FIRST EDITION

LIBRARY OF CONGRESS CATALOG CARD NUMBER: 71-148438

Contents

TO S. H. BONSU ABBAN
of the University College of Ghana—
Killed in an Air Crash When Journeying to Bring
East and West Together Through Religion

and

TO MAKERERE UNIVERSITY COLLEGE,
Kampala, Uganda, Mother University of East Africa

Preface

There are four main characters in the drama of the history of religions in Africa. There is Christian, who was born of Jewish stock around the beginning of our era and soon made his appearance on the African continent. He was enthusiastically received and became a citizen in the countries we now call Egypt, Sudan, Ethiopia, Libya, Tunisia, Algeria, and Morocco. Secondly there is Muslim, who was born in Arabia and came to Africa as a lusty young stripling, quickly to win the heart of most of the countries just mentioned. In all of them except Ethiopia and parts of Egypt the first gentleman was forgotten. Muslim undertook the long march across the Sahara and into the grasslands further south. He began to pay court to Black Africa. We now perceive that the third of our characters has been there all the time. It is difficult to find her a worthy name; some Nigerian students call her "A.T.R." pronounced "Atiar," from the initial letters of "African Traditional Religions." (If that sounds like an African political party, the abbreviation used by Ugandans, "Aftrad," sounds like a United Nations subsection.) That she cannot be given one slick label, that she does not talk as much as the others, but *is,* has its own significance.

We next see Christian in the fifteenth century coming down the coasts of Africa. His Oriental origins are hardly discernible; he is a highly Westernized gentleman now. Once again he is generously received, but somehow his presence fades. In the meantime Muslim has made himself at home right across the grasslands of Africa from the Atlantic to the Indian Ocean and is having adventures in the forests.

In the nineteenth century both Christian and Muslim find their way into the rest of Africa. Somehow the Traditional Religions survive their caveman methods of love-making as well as the strange new forces they bring with them. The three religions play their parts in the colonial era and the regaining of African independence, and we glance toward their future roles.

The task before us is to visualize Christianity and Islam in the African environment; it is an attempt in the ecology of religion, in the etymological sense of that word, a study of the thing in its African household or home, in its wholeness, in its total habitat. There is bound to be something of the peeping Tom here. No one knows what a religion really is; each religion has to come to a new environment in the garments of the sending culture. As a religion changes, we may get a glimpse of her as she really is, or if she refuses to change, we can tell that the clothes have become the person. One who has studied Islam in India and Pakistan learns a great deal about the essence of Islam by studying Islam in Africa. Someone who has studied the Christianity of Europe and the United States will be taught many things by African Christianity.

Mrs. Malaprop rightly said "caparisons is odious." Much comparative religion may be dubbed in her sense "caparisons of religion." In a study like this it is difficult to avoid giving an impression of *tu quoque*—"and you too." "Muslim slavery was bad, but ho! ho! ho! Christian was *much* worse." God makes himself known to men in every religion who seek him; evidence of his grace and blessing is to be found in every faith. Yet there is in every religion the human element which is the vehicle of the divine. There is also in each the diabolical. The student of religions has to learn discernment accordingly, he has to enter into each religious world view with love, respect, and humility, but not abandon his critical faculty. We are here studying "theology," the Word of God, through the history of these religions; as well as "anthropology," the study of Man; and "psychology," the study of *the* soul, the spirit of Being and Man—all in the African setting.

This book is also the attempt to convey in writing something of an adventure in study which began in the 1950's, when a Department of Theology was opened at the University College of the Gold Coast (Ghana). The first professor, J. P. Hickinbotham, with his colleagues, S. G. Williamson and C. G. Baeta, began a lecture series on the History of Christian Expansion, and they also began teaching the Study of African Traditional Religion and of Islam. In January 1956 the present writer joined in the work. By this time it was possible to make much more extensive use of student participation and to call in visiting experts. In the meantime F. B. Welbourn at Makerere University College in Uganda had begun work in the Traditional Religions, Christianity, Islam, and the "rebel" churches. He encouraged undergraduate students to collect field material, believing that even without extensive training, since they came mostly from the peoples being studied, the material they brought in was well worth collecting before it was lost. In 1963 Mr. Welbourn was joined by the writer and over the years by Messrs. Eric Hutchison, John Mbiti, Said Hamdun, Aloysius Lugira, Philip Turner, and Miss Louise Pirouet. A full set of courses in African Traditional Religion, the History of Islam and of Christianity in Africa, and Religion in Contemporary Africa could now be offered. Graduate work was started. The technique employed was to encourage students who showed a particular interest in a topic or area of study to read and think around it, discuss it in the residence hall, and go and visit the locality and talk with people there. Then at the end of a term (quarter), to gather a group who might be interested, give them an outline of contents, and discuss the kinds of projects that might be prepared for or attempted. When the term opened, the faculty would begin a short series of discussions on what they thought the topic really was and which books and techniques would help or hinder. More definite projects were chosen by the students and discussed by the group. The faculty now began to present their material —defining a topic, stating their method, arguing "on the one hand" then "on the other," and giving "a balanced conclusion." This was analytically and critically considered by the group. Student projects began to come in: book reports, essays on a cerebral theme, select translations with notes from languages such as Swahili and Luganda, descriptions of matters investigated on the ground, student-conducted tours by bus and on foot of holy places (referred to as church and mosque crawling). There were tapes and photographs of ceremonies and interviews with "knowing ones." The visit of a practicing "witch-finder" was of great service. That most useful of university experiences, the honest positive negative, came up not infrequently. With good humor we all learnt to recognize—whether the perpetrator was staff or student or visitor—intellectual hypocrisy, shoddy work, and the shortchanging of the academic customer—but knew we had to live with it and were ourselves adepts.

In 1968 the writer moved to the newest campus of the University of California amongst woods and meadows overlooking the Pacific. He was eager to see in what ways experience in the Study of Religions gained on one continent can be adapted for use on another. The University of California most liberally allows students to do independent studies under faculty supervision. A number of the themes discussed in this book have had the benefit of adoption for study by generous young Californians. California students have also contributed to the book through their discussion during a quarter course (which included the Cambodia strike) on "Christianity and Islam in Africa," given jointly by Dr. A. M. Lugira of Makerere and the writer.* Care has been taken not to steal Dr. Lugira's material, though living close to a friend over a period of years makes it difficult not to be saturated by his thought.

Inevitably many topics will be raised for discussion and left inconclusively in the air. Other vital topics are most adequately discussed elsewhere, so they are arbitrarily not raised at all. There are numerous *non sequiturs,* caused by the fact that the writer's notes and thoughts have been jumbled by earlier attempts in 1962 and 1966 with different objects, much moving, and university activity of a nonacademic nature having chiefly to do with the fullness of life in new residential colleges. Above all, the material is thoroughly recalcitrant and intractable. Try arranging it as straight chronicle and the attempt dies of sheer size and boredom. Making it into a series of biographies is thrilling but utterly bewildering to the reader. The "history of religious thought" approach discloses how threadbare a writer's own

*Dr. Lugira was enabled to visit us thanks to the generosity of Mr. Charles E. Merrill, Jr. and the University of California.

thinking is. In the end, I have put in bits of each approach and superimposed bright ideas as to methods of "doing one's own thing" in the history of religions.

In a previous book, *Religions of Africa—A Pilgrimage into Traditional Religions* (New York: Harper & Row, 1970), I have tried to set down the characteristic features of four traditional religions and discussed examples of master topics which appear in most traditional religions—sacral people and the ceremonies of life's turning points. Though the present volume is complete in itself, it follows on from the earlier work and takes up some of its themes to examine them in the environment of the modern Western world which has broken into Africa. Thus we see some of the sacral African monarchs (male and female) surviving the colonial regime, to be abolished by modern presidents who however take over some of the cultus of divine kingship.

Like its predecessor, this book is, hopefully, an *instrumentum studiorum,* a tool for use by the reader. He or she is asked to enter into the picture, to visualize Christianity and Islam coming into the African environment, to try to work out what happened to them there and to the matrix religion, to try to envisage their way ahead into the future and their peculiar contribution to humanity and world religions. It is possible that the reader may meditate on the subjects raised and perhaps gain an inkling of our fourth main character, a Lord of History and of Revelation, communicating through books and events, things and people. He is self-limited by their capacity to convey, and the freedom of man. There are, however, so many man-made horrors and opportunities missed, he may well side with the atheists and prefer to be ignored.

It remains to thank the many generous friends who have helped with this book at various stages and in sundry ways. Their names ("alphabetized, without title" in the bluff California way) include: Omar Abdullah, J. W. T. Allen, J. Omosade Awolalu, Christian Baeta, Jerome Bamunoba, Rohit Barot, Cyprian Bamwoze, Tom Beetham, Philip Bell, Leslie Brown, Edmund Burke IV, Alan and Clare Claydon, Don Cutler, Peter Dagadu, Kwesi Dickson, Mohammed el Dessuky, Philip Ehrensaft, Caroline Elliott, Walter Fischel, Colin Forrester-Paton, Edward Fasholé-Luke, Humphrey Fisher, Hannah Gathi, Madelaine Githae, Hans-Werner Gensichen, Ahmad Taha

al-Hadad, Said Hamdun, Holger Hansen, Adrian Hastings, Marguer-
ite Hermann, Vera Hodgson, Eric Hutchison, Israel 'Ibuoye, John
Isbister, Bandali Sherali Jaffer, Eleanor Jordan, Prince Badru Kakun-
gulu, S. A. Kamali, David Kamilu, Abdul Kasozi, John Kesby,
Samula Kimuli, Evelyn King, Francis King, Jan Knappert, Francis
Kokuma, Beverly Lancaster, Annabel Learned, Aloysius Lugira,
Hakim Lukhman, John Markham, Abubakr Mayanja, Francis X.
Mbazira, John Mbiti, Amim Mutabya, Azim Nanji, Shabaan Nkutu,
Ahmed Khab Nsambu, Dunstan Nsubuga, John Nsubuga, Rudolph
Nyako, Arye Oded, James O'Connell, Louise Pirouet, John Pobee,
Roy Poucher, Akhtar Rizvi, Ian Roach, Harry Sawyerr, Shuaib
Semakula, Bolaji Idowu, Harold Turner, Philip Turner, Andrew
Walls, Fred Welbourn, Gavin White, Trevor Williams, S. G. William-
son and Mercy Yamoah. Apologies are extended to the many others
not mentioned. Books like this make enemies for the author and no
friends. No friend nor other should be held responsible for the writer's
mistakes, bad recording and misunderstandings. It is a pleasure to
thank Dorothy Bergen, who typed the manuscript; the librarians at
Legon, Makerere, and Santa Cruz who sought out books near and far;
Christopher Francis and other friends at Blackwells at Oxford whose
catalogs have assisted me in teaching these last twenty years; and the
Research Committees of those three universities as well as the Rocke-
feller and Spalding Foundations and the Theological Education Fund,
which gave grants for work and travel of which this book is the
by-product.

N. Q. KING

University of California, Santa Cruz
Lakshmi Puja and Thanksgiving Day, 1970

CHRISTIAN AND MUSLIM IN AFRICA

CHAPTER ONE

The Tenderness of the Espousals-Christianity First Comes to Africa

1. THE EGYPTIAN CHURCH

Both Christianity and Islam can claim to have entered the African continent during the earliest days of their existence. A modern Ugandan Christian will tell you that water from his country goes down the Nile to Egypt, and there the Blessed Virgin, St. Joseph, and the Holy Child drank of it. A modern Egyptian Christian will explain that his Coptic Church (the word "Coptic" comes from the Greek for "Egyptian") was founded by St. Mark, secretary to St. Peter not many years after the resurrection of Jesus. When Eusebius, the first church historian, came to write his great work early in the fourth century, one of his main centers of interest was this church in Egypt, which was then amongst the oldest and most important in the world. Papyrus scraps and archeological remains show us that by the end of the second century Christianity had penetrated far inland, and that Egypt was one of the first countries where a majority of the rural folk became Christian—centuries before south Italy or France. For longevity of tradition and continuity in the same locality, the church in Egypt is surpassed perhaps only by Rome. Beside it the church in England is a stripling and the church in America a child.

For obstinate survival against all forms of coercion, the Egyptian

1

church is perhaps only surpassed by the Jewish people. For the first four centuries the worst persecutions of Christians by pagan Roman emperors occurred in Egypt. When the emperors decided to become Christian they took it upon themselves to tell church people what orthodoxy was. From Constantine to Justinian—that is, from the fourth to the sixth centuries— the emperors found in Christian Egypt an intractable opposition. When the Arabs took Egypt (639–641), the Copts welcomed the Muslims as a pleasant change from their persecuting Byzantine imperial coreligionists and for two centuries had a kind of golden age. But sporadic outbursts by fanatical crowds, as well as bouts of madness among the ruling class, created a cycle of persecution followed by uneasy peace which went on repetitively till the nineteenth century.

The early church in Egypt produced a succession of theological thinkers who dominated the world church of the day and are still important. There was Origen, who died in about 254 A.D. His name has some connection with the old African god Horus. As a young man he wanted to join his father in prison so as to be martyred with him, but his mother, fearing to lose at once both breadwinners for a numerous family, hid his clothes. His lectures and classes made him one of the most popular teachers in Alexandria, a city famous for its higher education. Some early historical sources suggest that, in an excess of zeal and to prevent any scandal (since he had many women students), Origen took literally the saying of Jesus that some make themselves eunuchs for the Kingdom of God's sake. As his fame as a teacher and thinker mounted, he visited churches outside Egypt and incurred the jealousy of his bishop. He settled down in nearby Caesarea in Palestine. His works on the Bible, the Trinity, and Christ, on the overcoming of sin and death and many other themes, have found a permanent place in Christianity, even though some of his ideas were later condemned. He died as a result of ill-treatment received during persecution.

Arius of Alexandria (who died around 336 A.D.) developed one side of Origen's thought and produced a doctrine of the Trinity which haunted the church at large for centuries. Another man from Egypt, St. Athanasius (d. 373), was one of the main proponents of an opposite point of view, which has become definitive for the world church. St. Cyril of Alexandria (d. 444) set forth the main features of the church's doctrine of Christ, while his successor Dioscorus upheld views that helped to cause a schism which has lasted to this day.

Besides these major fathers and heretics ("Dads and Bads" as the Oxford student calls them), Christianity produced a phenomenal amount of what we would call "the occult." Magical formulae and invocations abound among the papyri. "Gnostic" groups flourished. Many of these believed that the earth was the center of a system of planets, each with its influence and guardian, and that the soul is a light particle imprisoned in the body, which is its tomb. Salvation they thought of as a rescue from this imprisonment through esoteric knowledge. Remnants of the old Egyptian religion, together with migrant elements from the East—perhaps some Hindu, certainly some Manichean—found a certain hospitality amongst Christians in Egypt.

Some of these experiments with new and bizarre ways of doing things led to Christian Egypt being the mother of monasticism. The Bible speaks much of love and community. Early Christianity spoke of asceticism and chastity. In Egypt the Christians combined these ideas with elements from Jewish, Hellenistic, and Oriental sources to try out monasticism as a way of life in which love, sex, joy, togetherness, holiness, asceticism, prayer, meditation, and fasting could be practiced under utopian conditions in the wilderness of the desert. This gift of the church in Egypt, the organized religious community, was the instrument the church used to convert and civilize the barbarians of the north, especially in such dark regions as England, Germany, and Russia. It has left no small mark for good and ill in places such as Latin America, California, and the Philippines.

A study of the history of Coptic art reveals yet other glories of this church. She was not afraid to take over motifs from the old Egyptian religion and from Hellenism. The ideal statue-form of the Holy Mother Isis in her blue robe, and her divine infant Horus, became a standard Christian nativity setting. The *ankh,* the hieroglyph for life, was combined with the cross in iconography to be a symbol of resurrection after death.

In her golden age in the first years of Muslim rule (the seventh to ninth centuries), the Coptic Church was among the most flourishing in the world. The densely populated countryside of Egypt was hers; she had an art, liturgy, and theology which went deep into the lives of the people. Coptic scholars were sharing in the task of teaching the wisdom of the Greeks to the Arabs, who would in their turn help to teach the Europeans. Coptic physicians and administrators were serving in many parts of the Muslim world and were free to travel from Spain to Sind. Thanks to the administrative genius of men like Athanasius and Cyril—who besides being mystics and saints were intensely practical men, not above letting their more muscular supporters beat up troublesome opponents—the church in Egypt was one of the richest and best-organized corporations in the world, with a good measure of democratic control and a career open to talent. A member of it could be sure of help and opportunity, whether his need or capacity was spiritual, physical, social, or domestic. The Coptic Church had already enjoyed a long and distinguished history. Before her lay the long attrition of the centuries: her numbers dwindled as people left her for the manifest advantages of being Muslims in a Muslim world. Yet she has triumphantly survived. As the modern pilgrim prays in one of her churches, a blank wall to the outside but all beauty within, he is bound to marvel at the strength of the Coptic Christian will to survive, and the tolerance of Islam to these people of the Book. Regarding this the Muslim Egyptian diplomat who was showing us around remarked: "Was not Maryam, that lady so loved by the Prophet, a Copt? And have we not been together since the beginning?"

2. THE CHURCH IN ROMAN AFRICA

From Egypt away to the northwest of the continent lay Roman Africa. This included Africa proper—that is, the area now in Tunisia from which the continent derives its name, as well as parts of the countries we would now call Algeria and Morocco, north of the Sahara. No one knows when Christianity was first brought there. By the end of the second century it was well established. Here is a contemporary account of the trial, held at Carthage in 180 A.D., of a group of people arrested at Scili, a few miles from there.

> Speratus, Nartzalus, Cittinus, Donata, Secunda, and Vestia were on trial. Saturninus the Proconsul said: "You may obtain the indulgence of our Lord the Emperor if you

return to a good attitude of mind."

Speratus said: "We have never done wrong, we have never yielded ourselves to any deed of iniquity, we have never cursed, but when badly done by we have given thanks: because we reverence our Emperor."

Saturninus the Proconsul said: "But we also are religious, and our religion is simple: we swear by the genius of our Lord the Emperor, and supplicate for his health, which also you too should do."

Speratus said: "If quietly you will lend me your ears, I tell you a mystery of simplicity."

Saturninus said: "When you begin to speak evil of our sacred things, I shall not lend you my ears; but rather, you swear by the genius of our Lord the Emperor!"

Speratus said: "I do not know a dominion of this age; but rather I serve that God whom no man ever saw, nor is able with these eyes to see. I have done no theft; but if I buy anything, I pay the tax; because I recognize my Lord, the King of Kings and Emperor of all peoples."

Saturninus the Proconsul said to the other accused: "Cease being of this persuasion."

Speratus said: "It is an evil persuasion to do murder, to bear false witness."

Saturninus the Proconsul said: "Do not be partners in this madness."

Cittinus said: "We have no one to fear other than our Lord God who is in the heavens."

Donata said: "Honor Caesar as Caesar, but fear God."

Vestia said: "I am a Christian" [*Christiana sum*].

Secunda said: "What I am, that is what I want to be."

Saturninus the Proconsul said to Speratus: "Do you persevere in being a Christian?"

Speratus said: "I am a Christian." [*Christianus sum*] (And with him all the others were in consensus.)

Saturninus the Proconsul said: "Do you wish for a space of time to think it over?"

Speratus said: "There is no thinking over in a matter as righteous as this."

Saturninus the Proconsul said: "What are the things in your bag?"

Speratus said: "Books and letters of Paul, a just man."

Saturninus the Proconsul said: "Have a delay of thirty days and think it over."

Speratus again said: "I am a Christian." (And with him they all agreed.)

Saturninus read out the sentence from a writing tablet: "Speratus, Nartzalus, Cittinus, Donata, Vestia, Secunda, and the others, having confessed that they live according to the Christian rite, although the opportunity has been offered to them to return to the custom of the Romans and they have obstinately persisted, it is decided that they be put to the sword."

Speratus said: "We give thanks to God."

Nartzalus said: "Today we are martyrs in the heavens; thanks be to God."

Saturninus the Proconsul commanded that it should be announced by a herald: "Speratus, Nartzalus, Cittinus, Veturius, Felix, Aquilinus, Laetantius, Januaria, Generosa, Vestia, Donata, and Secunda I have ordered to be led out to execution."

One and all said: "Thanks to God."

Christiana sum, Christianus sum—"I am a Christian"—thus typically enough speaks one of the earliest pieces of the recorded history of the church in Africa. The new religion spread rapidly and went deep. It was Roman Africa that produced some of the greatest thinkers of Latin or Western Christianity, which is the only form of Christianity most of us know today. It was Tertullian from Carthage (d. about 220 A.D.) who hammered out the phrases that shape the Roman Catholic, Lutheran, Episcopalian, Presbyterian, and Methodist orthodoxy concerning the Trinity and the doctrine of Christ. It was Cyprian of Carthage (d. 258) whose views on the church still dominate many thinkers in those churches. It was Augustine of Hippo (354–430), whose mother Monica bore a name honoring an old African goddess, whose thought has brooded for good and ill over much of the European mind ever since. Perhaps if Augustine had experienced sexual intercourse within the bonds of a happy marriage, or had a less dominating mother, Freud would have found less to do. When some Ghanaian ecclesiastical students once complained that the missionaries tried to bind them with doctrines imported from outside Africa, a student from the university laughingly reminded them that many of the doctrines brought from Europe were only regurgitated reexports.

The church in Roman Africa was full of life and driving power. Inevitably she produced factions and divisions. Unfortunately she produced no mechanism for genuine reconciliation or pragmatic coexistence. In the middle of a fierce controversy someone would appeal to the civil power. We even find Augustine twisting the meaning of the Parable of the Wedding Guests to say that people must be *compelled* to come in. The Roman "Christian" state had gone quite far in the foul work of compelling all Christians to conform to state orthodoxy, when some Germanic barbarians broke in—the Vandals —and wrecked the economy of the country. Then the East Romans reconquered and reasserted the compulsion. When the Muslims came up in the seventh century they met with strong initial resistance. Over the years the Berber people went over to Islam, the Greco-Romans of the coast faded out, perhaps by taking ship to Sicily and Italy. In the eleventh and twelfth centuries Normans and other Christians from Europe found some surviving congregations, but in the end Christianity died out here utterly and completely, in a way which did not happen in other Christian heartland countries overrun by Islam, such as Egypt, Palestine, Syria, or Asia Minor. (Turkey was no longer a Muslim country as such when in our own day the Christians—more because they were Greeks than because they were Christian—were driven out of Asia Minor.)

Christian Roman Africa gave the universal church, and hence the world at large, many a gift. Modern students of the church in Africa like to point out that just as Islam was coming up to Roman Africa, the pope of Rome invited Hadrian, an "African by nation" as Bede puts it, to go to Britain as head of the church. He was well versed in sacred letters (that is, he was a scholar of the Bible), experienced in ecclesiastical and monastic affairs, and most learned in Greek and Latin. The African declined the honor, perhaps because the rushing life of a missionary bishop in a far bush country was not for him.

However, he consented to go as head of the monastery and college at Canterbury. From 670 A.D. for thirty-nine years he worked among the barbarian Anglo-Saxons, being especially zealous to set up schools and to keep the native church in line with the mother church overseas.

As a modern pilgrim to the Christian holy places of North Africa kneels amidst the ruins of a many-pillared basilica by the sea, or looks out across an old city on the plateau which gave its name to some church council of long ago, he will wonder how Christianity could disappear so completely. This is a land which eats up churches. Some scholars blame the church of Roman Africa for remaining so foreign. Every time there was a movement which might really have made Christianity thoroughly native, people with foreign connections "brought the church round." Others blame her for her factiousness. Some say that as the people went all too rapidly (and without understanding the complete difference) from their ancient gods—old Saturn, who was a kind of Baal or Moloch demanding a child—to a God before whose wrath man's sin was covered by the gift of his own Son, so they moved on easily to an Allah whose Prophet could be given the role of a Christ. The main reason for the disappearance of Christianity in the northwest of the African continent may well have been the beauty of in-coming young Islam, compared with the tired Christianity left by the great struggle between Catholics and the others, eking out an existence in a society ruined by barbarian invasion and East Roman reconquest.

3. THE CHURCH IN NUBIA

South of Egypt along the Nile up to the confluence of the Blue and the White Nile, in the area we now call Khartoum in the Sudan, lay the Nubian kingdoms. A large part of this area is being flooded as a result of the building of the Aswan High Dam and the creation of Lake Nasser. The findings of the archeological expeditions organized by the United Nations to save the monuments before flooding will take years to be published in full, but we already have a fair picture of these medieval Nubian Christian kingdoms. It has been suggested that the Ethiopian eunuch, "an officer of Queen Candace," who, according to the Book of Acts (chapter 8) was converted by the deacon Philip and returned home rejoicing, came from the kingdom of Meroë, which lay on the Nile somewhat south of Egypt. Since there was constant contact between Egypt and the south, it is likely that Christianity filtered through to the Nubian lands in the fourth and fifth centuries. From the sixth comes an account in Syriac of how the East Roman Emperor Justinian (d. 565) and the Empress Theodora sent expeditions to Nubia. The Emperor's mission was held up by the border officials on the Empress' instructions and her group went ahead. The mission met with great success, even though it was so hot there that the missionary sometimes sat in water in a subterranean place and thus went on with his teaching.

When the Muslims occupied Egypt and came south in the 640's they found the local Christians excellent fighters ("eye-smiters" they called them), and made a pact. The churches in Nubia lived on and prospered. In the ninth, tenth, and eleventh centuries Christianity in Nubia could be ranked amongst the healthiest on earth. Elsewhere Mesopotamian Christianity had crossed the roof of the world to China and was making steady progress along the great Asian trade routes. In India the church which looked back to St. Thomas as its founder was already entering its long preservative sleep. (The writer's parents came from the Mount of St. Thomas in South India.) In Palestine and Syria the local Christians were soon to face the unhelpful intrusion of the Crusades. In eastern Europe the Orthodox Church centered in Constantinople was holding out against Islam to the east and seeking to convert the barbarians such as the Slavs around her. The Latin church was just emerging from the Dark Ages and pushing on into northern Europe as the Celtic church began to decline.

The church in Nubia developed a Christian architecture and art of its own suited to and redolent of the country. It seems to have tolerated ancient customs such as the "Pharaonic circumcision" and infibulation of girls. A thorough analysis of Nubian Christianity's relationship to Black African religious traditions and to the old Egyptian gods has still to be made. Nubian Christian influence seems to have reached westward perhaps as far as the Lake Chad area. Nubian pilgrims went to Jerusalem, and some intermittent contact was kept up with Greek Christianity.

As the centuries wore on, Christianity slowly died out in Nubia. From Khartoum airport a visitor can take a Land Rover to the ruins of Soba, one of that faith's last strongholds in Nubia. The friendly

Muslim curator said as the visitor rose from his prayers, "You prayed that once again the church in the Sudan may be strong. May Allah grant your prayer, for Muslims and Christians should live at peace together." It is good for people studying the life and death of churches (and we may subsume most religious congregations under that title for the purpose of such musings) to reflect on the ecology of churches. Like redwood trees, if the climate changes too drastically, or if clumps are thinned too far, or if the ax and an artificially arid surface are too liberally present, they die. But the strange thing is that the Lord of the whole proceedings does not guarantee the survival of any group. In fact he fairly deliberately moves them out of their place if they fail to meet his requirements for life. It is true that he causes other clumps to spring up elsewhere, but that is another story. Perhaps it is too imaginative to think of the churches among the Dinka and Nuer and the black peoples of the southern Sudan as being the spiritual heirs of Christian Nubia.

4. THE CHURCH IN ETHIOPIA

Outside the post office in Addis Ababa a local artist will sell you a kind of strip cartoon depicting the story of how the Queen of Sheba (who is taken to be an ancestress of the present Emperor) went to visit King Solomon. He gave her a great feast, and since it was too late for her to return to her lodgings, she stayed the night in his palace. He wanted to lie with her, but agreed that he would not so long as she took nothing vital of his. The food had been salty, so when she thought the King was asleep she went to drink water from a jar he had set nearby. The King seized her hand—was not water vital? She consented to pay the forfeit and drank, and their child became the ancestor of the "Lions of Judah" who sit upon the Ethiopian throne.

The Ethiopians had some long-standing connection with Judaism, or at least with some Semitic religion. The Falasha, the so-called Ethiopian Jews, are a great puzzle to scholars; one explanation may be that they are the original substratum onto which Christianity was grafted. However this may be, the Ethiopians retain such customs as circumcision and ritual avoidances of women in menstruation and after childbirth.

There was some contact between Ethiopia and Jerusalem in New

Testament times, though there is much confusion over the word "Ethiopia" since it seems to have been used vaguely of a large part of Africa. In the fourth century we come to firm historical material. An inscription tells us that King Ezana of Ethiopia left worshiping many gods to follow one God. In the same century the Latin historian Rufinus tells how two Christian youths from Syria voyaged to India. They came ashore in Ethiopia for provisions. After the massacre of their main party they were taken captive, and grew up at the Ethiopian court. Later, when one journeyed through Egypt he asked Athanasius, Patriarch of Alexandria, to send a bishop to Ethiopia. Athanasius thought no one could be more suitable than his informant, and so consecrated him and sent him back. The head of the Ethiopian church until recent times has always come from Egypt. This gave the church, though it came to be a Christian island in a Muslim sea, some kind of international contact, but it also meant that it often lacked leadership when the Abuna (Patriarch) was old or while they awaited the coming of another. There are those who would say that no church can afford always to have a foreigner as its head. In practice the real head of the church was often that other sacral person—the Emperor. Great saints have fought to prove that the head of state cannot be head of the church—Ambrose, John Chrysostom, Thomas Becket, Sir Thomas More, Bonhoeffer—but in the context of an African kingdom one sees that this is a revolutionary idea, for the king persons forth the corporate being of the people as a whole, and naturally he assists with, and if necessary controls, religion.

Another feature of the Ethiopian church is the vigor of its monasticism. Tradition has it that monks came from Syria; some would come regularly through the centuries from Egypt; but monasticism seems rapidly to have become indigenous. Each district had its community of monks, where some person eminent in austerity and holiness would gain a name as a saint and a doer of good. The parish clergy were often married men intimately associated with the locality. They and the choirmen maintained the cycle of weekly worship and yearly festivals, and it would seem that a local type of chanting, drumming, and dancing before the Lord was developed during the centuries. This was a type of Christianity that Westerners were afterward to find strange. As a daughter of Alexandria, the church in Ethiopia shared Egypt's separation from Rome over certain points of doctrine. Yet Ethiopian

Christianity was sturdy and independent and capable of surviving among her mountains century after century. By the second half of the sixth century the Ethiopians had spread into south Arabia and had built a Christian sanctuary at San'a. Some intruders desecrated it by urinating in it in unison, and in retaliation the Ethiopian viceroy went against an Arab sanctuary, the Ka'aba at Mecca, with elephants. He was turned back by some miraculous visitation. This took place in about the year 570 A.D., which is called by the Arabs "the year of the elephant." It was in this year that the Prophet was born.

CHAPTER TWO

Islam's Long March and Christianity's Second Attempt

1. THE COMING OF ISLAM TO ETHIOPIA AND EGYPT

Not many years after Uganda's independence in 1962, the Emperor Haile Selaisse of Ethiopia paid a state visit to Kampala. A delegation of local Muslims waited upon him to greet and welcome him. They read him a long speech in which they recalled that Bilal, the first muezzin (caller to prayer) had been an African, and that African voices had ever since called men everywhere to piety and religion. They referred to the fact that before his hegira from Mecca (in 622 A.D.) the Prophet Muhammad had sent a group of the first Muslims to Ethiopia to take refuge from the enemies of true religion. The Negus, the Emperor of Ethiopia, his great ancestor, had received them most graciously. The Prophet had blessed the Negus for this and prayed that he would never lack descendants on his throne. They knew that he (Haile Selaisse) in his turn and in his day was treating his Muslim subjects as full citizens with equal rights, and prayed that if so, his throne would remain secure.

Ever since those early days there have been Muslims in the horn of Africa (the northeastern coastlands jutting into the Red Sea and Indian Ocean) and Ethiopia. They have taken part in a peculiar love-hate relationship with Ethiopian Christians. For centuries the two

13

groups live in peace and mutual harmony, and then there is a life-and-death clash, when one opponent or the other is saved by a miracle. During the 1950's and 1960's, so it is hinted among Muslims in East Africa, the lot of the Muslims in Ethiopia has not been a happy one. Perhaps the speech of the Uganda Muslims touched something in the Emperor's conscience.

Some of those early Muslims stayed on in Ethiopia. As for the Ethiopian power structure in southern Arabia, it was demolished as Muslim power increased. By the end of the seventh century the Christians were being pushed back from the coast of the Red Sea, and gradually retreated to the mountains.

In Egypt the coming of Islam was much more spectacular. After the death of the Prophet in 632 A.D., the Muslim armies gathered in the Arabian peninsula and suddenly burst out to overcome the Persians in the Tigris-Euphrates region and the East Romans in Syria-Palestine. The leaders back in Mecca and Medina seemed to want to pause, but ᶜAmr Ibn al ᶜAs led a few hundred horsemen into Egypt and carried all before him. By 640 the Muslims had taken most of Egypt, and shortly after even the fortresses and the great seaport of Alexandria fell to them. Such a sudden, sweeping, and long-lasting victory has hardly been seen anywhere before or since. The conquerors did not set out to convert Egypt to Islam. They were content at first to live somewhat separately from the people, like a garrison, using local leadership and resources to run the country. The Copts could now come into their own, for the hated East Roman officials, tax collectors, imperialists, and so on had been ejected. Copts were craftsmen, secretaries, civil servants, and medical men for the Arabs. The Arabs respected their learning and began to study with them.

As the conquerors settled down they married local women. In Islam it is usual for a woman of another faith to join her husband's religion; or—if her people were people of the Book, Jews or Christians or Zoroastrians—she might retain her own faith, but her children followed their father's religion. In the early days of Islam, conditions were laid down concerning subject peoples. The peoples of the Book could remain in their religion, but they had to pay a tax for the protection Muslim arms gave them. They lost certain privileges—they could not serve as combat troops; sometimes they were not allowed to build new synagogues, temples, or churches; sometimes they had to wear special clothing and could not ride certain animals. However, various careers in the courts and palaces were open to them: notably, women of non-Muslim origin were taken into the harems of potentates and thus became the mothers of caliphs, sultans, and emperors. Islam showed a far greater tolerance for Christians and Jews than Christianity has shown for Muslims or Jews. But as the centuries wore on there were sporadic outbursts of persecution, while financial, political, and social pressures ground on relentlessly and Christians in greater numbers went over to Islam. Apostasy—that is, leaving Islam —carried the death penalty.

Islam slowly but surely gained ground in Egypt. Bit by bit Arabic became the language of the countryside as well as the towns; Coptic was preserved mainly in the liturgy of the church. Gradually the Coptic Church took on the aspects of the religion of a minority, inward-looking, sometimes proud to the point of arrogance, sometimes humble to the point of cringing, sometimes dreaming of an outside intervention, divine or human, sometimes more autochthonous than the most fiery nationalist in its art and music, in the homely piety of its womenfolk, surpassingly beautiful.

On the Muslim side, Egypt has remained to this day a powerhouse for Islam. This is particularly true of Egypt's place in Africa. Throughout the centuries her men have gone into Black Africa to travel, to trade, to build, to fight, to marry: together with these things, they have shown forth Islam. Black Africans going on pilgrimage or trading or traveling or studying have come to Egypt and learned more about the best in Islam there. Particularly one should recall in this context the great mosque-university of al-Azhar in Cairo, for in a way she is the mother university of the Western world.

Al-Azhar was founded in the tenth century, and even today it is impressive to see students from various parts of Muslim Africa (and significantly, Muslims of Black American origin) praying and studying among its *riwaks* (spaces between pillars allocated to different groups). In every generation al-Azhar has produced men well-trained in theology, the law, the exegesis of scripture, and the other Islamic sciences.

2. ISLAM COMES TO NORTHWEST AFRICA

After they had conquered Egypt in 640 A.D. the Muslim armies soon penetrated across Cyrenaica (in modern Libya), which had in its time produced Christian saints of the first rank, and began to probe the defenses of Roman Africa, Numidia, and Mauretania. One spectacular Arab conqueror reached the Atlantic and spurred his charger as far into the breakers as he could. Although this melodramatic gentleman was somewhat ignominiously killed on his way home, it was somehow a prophetic act. Owing to the ruthless fanaticism of Spain, Islam did not cross the Atlantic in the fifteenth and sixteenth centuries along with Christianity, but she may successfully do so in the twentieth.

The Muslims met the staunchest resistance in northwest Africa. The Berbers, who had survived centuries of domination by Phoenicians, Carthaginians, and Greco-Romans and had been influenced by Judaism and Christianity, opposed the Arabs for half a century. Yet many of them went with the Arabs to the conquest of Spain. Only with difficulty were the Muslims turned back in 732 A.D. when halfway across France. Spain became a Muslim country for seven hundred years. The last outpost of Islam in western Europe only surrendered in the year Columbus came to the New World. North Africa became Muslim through and through. It was called the Maghrib—the West, a kind of island between the sea and the desert. It, too, was a great powerhouse for Islam: Tunisia, Algeria, and Morocco have remained so to this day. There were world-renowned mosques and centers of religion and learning at places such as Tunis, Kairwan, and Fez.

Islam's "West" also produced men of world distinction. We may mention Abd al-Rahman Ibn Khaldun, who was born in Tunis in 1332 A.D. After a first-rate education he went to serve the sultan at Fez (in Morocco) as a courtier, diplomat, and judge, and then in various places such as Granada, Bougie (in Algeria), and Cairo. As was inevitable in that kind of work, he spent some time being thrown into prison and magnanimously released. He was a deeply religious man and performed the pilgrimage not only to Mecca but also to Jerusalem and to Bethlehem. He was a brilliant scholar and a master of research. His "Introduction to World History" remains a master-piece, for he tried by investigating historical facts to find whether there was a rhythm or pattern in the affairs of men. He was in a way an inheritor of the Jewish school of Deuteronomic historians and (more indirectly) of Herodotus and the Greeks. Islam gave him his basic thinking and his lucidity and rational logic of approach. He looks at man's attempts to organize himself at different stages till he reaches the urban community development. The factor holding this together is ^{c}*asabiyah,* "group togetherness," and when this decays a civilization falls apart. He finds his rhythm in the barbarians coming in, strong in togetherness; they become civilized by imitation of their predecessors, then decline as they lose their inner cohesion—to be replaced by other newcomers. The great man died in 1406, having experienced many griefs, including the drowning of his family at sea.

3. ACROSS THE SAHARA TO BLACK AFRICA

From these solid homelands in South Arabia, Egypt, and North Africa, Islam could spread into Black Africa. She could take centuries about it; there was no need for central control or drive, it could all happen naturally. The Sahara was not a barrier. It was like the sea, a difficult and awesome element which could be useful to those who had the skill to use it. In the East, Muslim navigators learned from their Indian and Persian Gulf predecessors how to use the monsoon winds. At a time when most European sailors hugged the coast, they could boldly set the rudder and drive across the high seas miles from land.

Arab geographers and historians have left descriptions of these adventures across deserts and sea. On the basis of these accounts and their own researches, scholars reconstruct the course and interrelation of events. Then other scholars may soon enjoy unlinking the facts and reassembling them another way. For the moment, the following is the generally received version of the story. In the eleventh century the various Berber tribes of the Sahara were becoming more and more thoroughly converted to Islam. Some of their leaders went on the pilgrimage to Mecca and brought back teachers. One such was Abdallah Ibn Yasin (d. 1059 A.D.), whose mother was of Berber descent. He tried to reform Islam in the western Sahara. He was bitterly disappointed, and is said to have withdrawn to a *ribat* or retreat somewhere on the Atlantic coast. It was a fortified place where people could give their time to study and devotion and preparing themselves to carry the faith to others. After some time the people of the *ribat* (the *murabitun,* hence "Almoravids," according to an etymology which seems too slick) sallied forth to raise Islam to higher levels. They swept up through North Africa into Spain. Their activities seem to have had some effect on events away to the southeast. In about 1076 A.D. the black kingdom of Ghana, where Muslims and followers of the Traditional Religions had lived side by side in a kind of dualism, disintegrated. At the capital there had been two towns; one was Muslim, with twelve mosques including a Friday mosque. Each had its prayer leader, caller to prayer, and reciters of the Qur'an. In this town were men learned in the law of Islam and her sciences. The non-Muslim town was six miles away, and there too was a place of prayer for the Muslim secretaries and officials.

One of the results of the breakup of old Ghana was that certain Islamized groups became itinerant traders and carried their faith with them toward the forests of the south. A group of merchants founded the city of Jenne around 1250 A.D. With Timbuktu (founded around 1100 A.D.), it was to become a great center of Muslim learning. Scholars and traders from these cities kept in close touch with the Muslim world of the Maghrib, Egypt, and Arabia. They also traveled, taught, traded, married, and begat children across Africa to Hausaland in Nigeria and to Ashanti in Ghana.

The scene of Muslim advance shifts eastward now to the coast of East Africa and the West African empire of Mali. It is a delight to come upon a firsthand account of how things were with Islam in both these areas in the fourteenth century, left us by a man who himself came from the African continent—Muhammad Ibn Abd Allah, called Abu Abd Allah Ibn Battuta of the Luwata (a Berber group) of Tangier. He was born in 1304 A.D., and in his young manhood set out on the pilgrimage to Mecca. He journeyed across Africa and then visited Arabia, Syria, Iraq, Persia, Turkestan, the Crimea, Constantinople, various lands which are now in southern Russia, and on to India, Sumatra, and China. He dictated his memoirs in a clear and attractive Arabic, and his own personality, "warts and all," shines through the account. He was first and foremost a good Muslim, and his Islam enhanced and permeated his natural manhood and humanity. He was full of curiosity, a lover of good and exotic foods, an appreciator of womanly beauty and virtue. (Some regret that this writer of a gastronomic Baedeker of the medieval African and Asian world was prevented by his religion from appreciating the drink.)

Ibn Battuta shows us the Maghrib, Cyrenaica, and Egypt as deeply Islamized countries, with a religion adapted in different places to the locality, but recognizably part of that great international and timeless body, the household of Islam. He made three visits to Black Africa. In 1326 A.D. he was in Egypt and wished to go to Mecca. He went up the Nile and then across the desert to Aidhab on the Red Sea coast, whence he intended to sail to Jeddah, the port for Mecca. He met the Beja tribe—a people who do not pass on inheritance to daughters, as against the Muslim upholding of a woman's right to some inheritance. Among them he found a mosque rich in *baraka* and a venerable sheikh who had claims to Moroccan royal descent.* At Aidhab he found the sea crossing impossible because of local warfare, so had to return to Cairo.

A year or two later (1329–30 A.D.) Ibn Battuta set sail from Jeddah and in a couple of days reached the African coast not far from the island of Sawakin. Again he met the Beja, as well as certain Arabs who had mixed with them, and discovered close connections in trade and marriage with Mecca. He found his way back to Arabia and then set off on a long East African journey in January 1330 A.D.

Four days out from Aden he came to Zeila. The people were Blacks and seemed to be deeply involved in the Muslim legal and theological movements of the day. Our explorer gave the world prize for stench to this town. He spent the night on his ship, though the sea was choppy. Another fifteen days of sailing brought him to Mogadishu in what we would call Somalia. He was given special treatment, since he was a religious scholar, and lodged in a house reserved for such men. On the Friday he attended the Friday Prayer. The ruler of the place spoke to him in Arabic, and then they went in procession to the palace. Over the king's head were carried four canopies of colored silk

---

* *Baraka* is an almost tangible form of blessing, localized in a person or place, which is often useful in healing or doing miracles. The strictest Muslims are sometimes suspicious of it as mere superstition and associate it with some of the accretions Islam has taken on, especially in the Maghrib.

—a touch reminiscent of African kingship in such places as Ghana. The ruler held men versed in Muslim law in high regard. In matters to do with Muslim law the *qadi* (judge) gave his verdict, while in other matters the members of the sultan's council passed judgment.

Ibn Battuta sailed on toward the land of the Sawahil, which means "coastland," and of the Zunuj. One cannot be quite sure of the meaning of the root *z-n-j;* perhaps it means "Blacks." Slaves from this area working in the Mesopotamian salt marshes staged a revolt from 868 to 883 A.D. which shook the throne of the Abbasid caliphs at Baghdad. Ibn Battuta visited the island of Mombasa, now the chief port of Kenya. He found the people were Shafite Muslims, religious, trustworthy, and righteous. Most of them, he reported, were extremely black.

He went on to Kilwa, which is located some distance south of the modern port of Dar-es-Salaam in Tanzania. He found it a beautiful and elegant city. Indeed, standing today among the ruins of its great mosque, one can believe it was among the most graceful cities ever built by man. In the fourteenth century it could have competed for sheer loveliness with any city in Italy. Our traveler found the sultan a humble man who honored scholars, men of piety as well as people who could claim membership in the family of the Prophet. He was careful to share out his goods in keeping with Muslim law. He maintained a holy war against the unbelievers round about and was the soul of generous giving. At Kilwa, Ibn Battuta learned that half a month's journey further south lay the town of Sofala (in modern Mozambique), where the Muslims traded for gold. However, he caught the returning monsoon and reached the Yemen in Arabia.

Years later Ibn Battuta returned home to North Africa. From there he visited Spain, and then in 1352 set out on his last great journey—across the Sahara to the land of the Blacks. Already the Muslims had penetrated down the west coast to the Senegal area and had played a part in the life and death of the kingdom of Ghana. Ibn Battuta went from Morocco across the Sahara to the kingdom of Mali. On the way he was entertained by an Islamic scholar whose brother he had met in China.

After a terrible journey across the desert, he reached the town of Iwalatan, which was the first district of the Blacks. They were able to leave their goods unprotected but safe in an open place while they went to pay their respects to the viceroy. He did not speak to them directly but through a spokesman—an Africa custom of sacral king-ship which Ibn Battuta took to come from contempt for white men. A symbolic meal of grain with honey and milk he misunderstood to be parsimonious hospitality. He was particularly upset by the lack of sexual jealousy among the Blacks. He found that they traced their genealogies through their mothers' brothers and passed on inheri-tance to the sons of sisters. The women did not veil themselves, and refused to accompany their husbands when they traveled. They had male friends outside the circle of father and brother, and did all this though they were regular in prayer and studied the law and learnt the Qur'an by heart. Once when he visited the *qadi* (Muslim judge), who was a scholar and had been to Mecca, he found him with a very beautiful young woman who neither veiled herself nor withdrew. Another time he visited a Muslim friend who had lived in Maghrib and knew the law, to find the latter's wife, in his presence, sitting on a bed chatting to a male companion. At another point he remarks that their slave women and young girls go around naked, exposing their private parts. During the great fast, which the Blacks carefully kept, he had seen naked girls carrying food into the palace ready for the evening break-fast. Among them he even noticed two daughters of the sultan with already developed breasts who had no clothes on.

Ibn Battuta makes some amends for his misunderstanding of his black hosts when he comes to devote a section to praising them. He knew of many Blacks who had been on the *hajj* to Mecca and refers to the famous pilgrimage of Mansa Musa in 1324–25 A.D. This king of Mali made a deep impression at the Holy Places, and in Cairo he spent so much gold as to cause an inflation. Early European maps depict him as a mighty African monarch holding a giant gold nugget. Ibn Battuta says there is little injustice among the Blacks, and there is peace and security in their country, nor do they seize the property of dead foreigners. So far as one can tell, they respected visiting scholars sufficiently not to give them any visa or tax problems. He found them careful about prayer and mosque attendance; they wore clean clothes on Friday for service and learnt their Qur'an by heart.

He speaks highly of a number of the Blacks who befriended him, especially of one Farba Sulaiman who was representative of the king at a town downriver from Timbuktu. In his house he found a book in Arabic by a Baghdadi author, for the Farba understood Arabic and had an Arabic-speaking secretary and even a slave girl from Damascus. He seems to have looked back with genuine admiration to the generous way in which the Blacks treated him. He was not the last white man to regret when he came that he had come, and then on leaving to look back with respect. Ibn Battuta even admits some of his mistakes. Thus he was disgusted with the manners of a Black who stood by when he was emptying his bowels, and only afterward realized that the man was making a barrier between him and a crocodile which was lying in wait.

Eventually Ibn Battuta crossed the Niger (he calls it the Nile) and went on to the capital of the king of the Blacks (Mali). Here he was hospitably received by the *qadi* (a Black who had made the pilgrimage to Mecca) and other local and foreign Muslims. In an earlier volume there is an attempt to describe some elements in African kingship. In Ibn Battuta's account we find some of these elements together with Muslim features coming in beside them. Thus the king walked slowly in procession, stopping often; we know from Ashanti custom that if he stumbled or touched the ground it was a catastrophe. Again, a spokesman spoke for him to the people and for them to him. Certain "poets," as Ibn Battuta calls them, in costumes of feathers with headdresses made to look like birds, recited the heroic deeds of his ancestors and exhorted him to virtue. He records a dispute between the king and his senior wife, the daughter of his mother's brother, who was by custom his partner in the kingship. The king was trying to make another wife, not of the royal family, his first lady. We may see here perhaps the foreign consort-type of queen, who owed her position to her marriage, trying to supplant the African woman-king type, who was a ruler in her own right. Alas for the omnipresence of male chauvinism, with its female fellow-travelers!

Ibn Battuta noticed a complete set of Muslim officials at court and witnessed the keeping of the Feast of Sacrifice and the Feast of Fast-breaking at Mali, with the king coming in solemn procession and performing a prayer and hearing a sermon. He saw the sultan do justice and right wrongs in Muslim style.

Ibn Battuta also visited Gao, which was later to become prominent in the kingdom of Songhai. He stayed at Timbuktu, but spends more time in his memoirs on remarkable stories and poets than on scholars and religion. He mentions that Nubia is still Christian. In 1353 A.D. he recrossed the Sahara in a caravan in which there were about six hundred slave women, and finally reached home territory early the following year, in a snowstorm.

After the decline of Mali, leadership in Muslim affairs passed to Songhai, a kingdom on the Niger east and south of Timbuktu which rose to eminence in the fifteenth century. The Askia Muhammad, who returned from the pilgrimage in 1497 A.D., built a hostel for black students at Mecca. Islam went deep in many parts of his kingdom. Most unfortunately, the Muslim rulers of Morocco, lured on by lust for gold, sent an expedition of gunmen across the desert who, in the 1590's, destroyed Songhai.

Further south and eastward, Hausaland had received Islam, but African Traditional Religion remained powerful and reasserted itself at intervals. On the borders of Lake Chad the kingdom of Kanem (which later became Kanem-Bornu) had been under Muslim influence since the eleventh century and in close touch with Tunis, Egypt, and Mecca, especially after the fall of Christian Nubia.

We must not think that the work of Islam is only to be associated with the names of the great empires which have been mentioned. After all, these emperors and rulers were intent on greatness, on getting rich and governing their people. Religion was not first and foremost their concern, although it came into everything they did. The spread of Islam should also be associated with much more humble persons, such as the groups of scholarly traders who moved out from Islamized areas into Upper Guinea, the Ivory Coast, to Salaga and Wa in modern Ghana, and to other places. It was with them that Islam really began to penetrate the forest areas of West Africa. They lived their own social life, marrying women of the countries where they were, but making them into Muslims and bringing up their children as good Muslims, educated in Muslim learning. They did not interfere in local politics to any great extent, and had a kind of special position when any local wars broke out. They traded over a vast area, exchanging the goods of the more northerly areas for the gold, cola nuts, and slaves of the south. Sometimes Muslim clerical families would offer their aid to groups that were going in to conquer certain areas. Oral tradition in northern Ghana still tells how the Gonja conquerors were met by a family of Muslim clerics who agreed to go forward with them, calling for God's blessing on what they were doing and advising them as they went along. They were rewarded by being placed in each capital that was set up by the Gonja, so that today we find in each of these capitals a ruler from the conquering family as well as a *malam* or Muslim cleric, and very often also a priest of the old religion of that place, whose special duty was to carry out observances connected with the earth and with the spirits of the ancestors.

African kingdoms of the grassland, such as Mossi, as well as forest kingdoms such as Ashanti and Dahomey, seem to have been resistant to Islam at this time. There have been many theories as to why this was. Some say that it was because the Muslims did not like the forest, and their horses could not survive the tsetse fly. Closer study and research have shown that, in fact, the Muslims did penetrate these kingdoms very deeply indeed, but no mass conversion took place for a number of reasons. In Ashanti we learn that the Kramo, the Muslim community, were used as advisers, scribes, and secretaries, and as people who made charms and amulets for the Ashanti rulers, but although the Muslims were allowed to make converts and exercise their religion with complete freedom, care was taken that the ruling classes as such were not converted, lest the general run of the public follow them. An Asantihene who was too friendly to Islam had to be destooled in 1802.

The autobiography of a certain Abu Bakr al-Sadik gives us some interesting sidelights on the state of affairs at that time and in earlier centuries. He was born at Timbuktu in 1790 into a clerical and trading family. While still a small boy he moved to Jenne and then down to Bouna in what we would now call the Ivory Coast. There he continued his studies; indeed, it seems there were a large number of these Muslim clerics there, able to communicate with one another across the savannah land of Africa, who kept connections with Muslim learning in Egypt and even Arabia. The trade they were carrying on seems to have been mainly in gold. The town of Bouna became involved in warfare, and the Ashanti came up through Bole, which is now in Ghana, crossed the River Volta, captured the young man, and took him away through the forest. On reaching the sea they sold him to some English sailors, who immediately put him in a boat, rowed out to their ship and took him away to Jamaica. Eventually he was freed and sent on an expedition back to Africa. His story gives a rare glimpse of the penetration and depth of Islam among certain families of the time.

4. WHAT WAS IMMIGRANT ISLAM LIKE?

Islam, in coming to the African continent, must have had a tremendous attraction of its own which made it difficult for a Christian or follower of African Traditional Religion (for which after this the Nigerian abbreviation "A.T.R." will be used) to resist. Since most English-speaking people know less about Islam than they do about Christianity, it is worth repeating the summary used by Muslim colleagues of the characteristic features of their faith.

Islam is said to have five pillars of duty. The first is to confess that there is one God, and Muhammad is his prophet. This bearing witness is of the essence of Islam. The oneness of God is basic: he is, and he is one—all else follows logically. The logic and rationality of all that follows on this fundamental premise—the all-pervading oneness of God—cannot fail to impress and often overwhelm the mind. The Prophet did not claim to his followers to be what Jesus was to his, yet his being, his power, his character and relationship with God and man, remain central. Islam is submission to God—it is hardly "Muhammadanism," if that is taken to imply a following of Muhammad as Christians follow Christ, yet to a believer Muhammad is a person who goes through life with one, accompanying and showing the way, encouraging, exhorting, rebuking, and ultimately rewarding.

The second duty in Islam is prayer—a Muslim is a man of prayer. He may have many private devotions and he may meditate upon the ninety and nine beautiful names of God and belong to a group of mystics, but above all he should pray formally five times a day after ritual ablution. On Fridays and the Great Festivals special prayers are offered.

The third pillar is that a Muslim should give a certain proportion of his possessions as alms to maintain the poor and needy, to defray the cost of good causes taken up by Islam in the country as a whole, and to maintain the fabric of Muslim organization.

That a Muslim should go on a pilgrimage at least once in his lifetime to the holy house at Mecca, if circumstances permit, is the fourth pillar of Islam. The visit to the holy places will purify his soul; there also he will learn of the world-wide nature of Islam and be able to take back new insights into the purity of his own religion.

The fifth distinctive feature of Islam is that a Muslim should, during the sacred month of Ramadan, refrain from letting anything pass his gullet from dawn to dusk. This is no easy matter, especially in hot countries when the rotating lunar calendar brings the month of fasting into the hot season. Muslims will tell you of the benefits of the fast —physically it disciplines and purifies, morally it teaches restraint and reminds of the needs of others, spiritually it uplifts the mind to God.

Some teachers of Islam include the jihad, the holy war, among the duties. There is an obligation for a Muslim to join in the struggle against unfaith, to assist in the task of bringing everybody into the sphere of the household of Islam. Various Muslim leaders have at different times called for a jihad, but this does not mean that a Muslim has to rise up and follow every such summons, nor does it mean that by this call Islam has been universally assisted in its spread, though at times it has been a useful rallying cry for the faithful.

Islam does not have a "creed" in the Christian sense, but it is possible to name some fairly standard points of doctrine which give an outline of Sunni belief.* A Muslim must believe in one God and must not associate anything or anyone with him. He believes in God's Angels and his Books. The Qur'an is a heavenly book communicated to the Prophet. One does not say "Muhammad says," but "Thus says the Most High," in quoting it. God also gave *Tawrat* (Torah) to Prophet Moses, *Zabur* (the Psalms) to King David, and *Injil* (Gospel) to Prophet Jesus. Muslims reverence these scriptures too, but insist that the Jews and Christians have multilated them. They recognise God's prophets, including Jesus as a prophet. Muslims believe that there will be a resurrection and a judgment. They believe in the *qadar* of God, that is, the inexorable decree, the right measuring-out to a man. "Fate" is a wrong translation; good and evil come from the *qadar*—God knows best. Muslims believe in the resurrection of the dead.

Muslims have a detailed system of sacred law, the *shari'a*, which

---

*Most Muslims in Africa belong to the Sunni group, that is, they follow the *sunna* or customary way of catholic Islam and do not accept a leader descended from the house of the Prophet as being authoritative in the way the Shia do.

regulates every aspect of their lives. Law is far more important than theology, which in Christendom was the queen of sciences. Within the general oneness of Islamic Sunni law there are differing schools of thought. For our purposes, it is sufficient to note that in East Africa from the coast to the White Nile at Pakwach, the Shafi school is supreme; in North and West Africa, in the main, the Maliki school is followed.

There are certain prohibitions in Islam. Pig must not be eaten and other animals should be properly slaughtered. Alcohol is not to be drunk, and some schools of thought question the general use of drums, tobacco, and some forms of art. The strictest Islam also prohibits usury, gambling, and various forms of luxury.

A word of explanation is necessary about the *turuq* (singular *tariqa*), the "confraternities" in Islam. They go back to the Sufi movement in Islam, a form of mysticism by which a group of people join together to get to know more about God and to follow in his way. Often the leading man, the sheikh or head, is given a great deal of devotion, and it is believed that he gives out a certain special blessing and power called *baraka*. It is usually taken that behind him, in unbroken sequence, there is a kind of apostolic succession back to the days of the Prophet himself and his son-in-law Ali. Under the head there is an organization radiating out from the mother house through various representatives in different places who keep the order well organized. The ordinary member of the brotherhood is usually given the title *talib* or *murid,* disciple or learner. There are various gatherings of the brotherhoods; for instance, there is the *zikr.* The brethren meet to carry out a devotion in which they repeat the name of God and his attributes and recite portions of the Qur'an, singing the praises of their sheikh and carrying out rhythmic movements and breathing exercises which sometimes lead on to ecstasy. Gradually, as a disciple learns more, he is initiated into various forms of deeper knowledge and makes various promises and vows.

Two of the brotherhoods demand further comment here. The first is the *tariqa* of the Qadiriyya. It was founded in Mesopotamia in the twelfth century, and it was claimed that the basic teaching of this brotherhood goes back to the truths the Archangel Gabriel told Hazrat Ali. It is very orthodox, with a deep respect for the law of Islam. Its members are usually humble men, given to charity with a certain measure of tolerance for other religions. In this confraternity one finds a great number of people who are prepared to discuss the relationship of one religion with another and to applaud the best in other religions, whatever they may be. This brotherhood came into the area of West Africa by the fourteenth century, and Timbuktu was one of its main centers. But members of the brotherhood are to be found throughout Africa: for instance, in the whole of North Africa, in Egypt, all over West Africa, the Sudan, Ethiopia, East Africa, and even in the Comoro Islands and Madagascar. The second is the *tariqa* of the Tijaniyya, which was founded in the late eighteenth century when Ahmed Ibn Muhammad al Tijani went on the *hajj*. There at Mecca he had a dream of the Prophet and received a revelation concerning his way for his people. The followers of this *tariqa* believe that they will be near the throne of God on the Day of Judgment.

In studying Islam in Northwest and West Africa the reader will come upon references to *maraboutisme,* that is, the following of a charismatic religious leader and the build-up of a personality cult which can include devotions at his burial place. A visitor to former French West Africa will find that leaders of this kind have played a considerable role in politics, groundnut growing, and social life, especially in colonial times. In many parts of the Muslim world, at village level, he will find that there are countless holy places devoted to the memory of saints of the past. It is difficult to assess the importance of such elements in the history of Islam in Africa. On the other hand, the student of religion as he visits with new Muslim congregations all over the continent cannot fail to be impressed by the way in which individuals and small groups nearly always adopt a regime of prayer, mysticism, and devotion to go along with the more public and formal observances mentioned earlier on. It produces in them great beauty of life. Perhaps from the beginning it was these "pious ones" who provided the growing edge of the religion.

Islam is patient and does not like to go in for hurry-hurry tactics. Usually Muslims are content to let people call themselves Muslims and leave their Islamicity to Allah, who alone can judge a man's sincerity. Thus all sorts of beliefs and practices can coexist with a careful keeping of the main points described above. Even if a reformer does not arise for a few centuries, reform inevitably comes in the end, either spectacularly or over a few generations. It is possible to judge the penetration of Islam in a given place by examining various features in the life of a people. Islam can affect their world view, their law; their political, social, and domestic life; their agriculture, cooking, commerce, clothing; their labor relations and technology. It is a grand and architectonic system.

5. CHRISTIANITY TRIES AGAIN IN AFRICA

In the fifteenth century Christianity in Nubia faded out. New invaders such as the Funj came, and the Christian ruling houses were destroyed. The peasantry, bit by bit, went over to Islam. We hear one of the last cries of Nubian Christianity in the description by a Western Christian who reached the Ethiopian court around 1520, of how Nubians came to ask for help, but the Ethiopians said they had not the necessary resources. The Ethiopian church was holding its own and perhaps expanding in some areas, but could not hope to spread into Black Africa as a whole. There are some who think Ethiopian knights from the southwestern areas with their chaplains reached parts of what we would today call Kenya and Uganda, and the nineteenth-century missionaries into the intra-lacustrine basin of East Africa kept finding what they thought were vestiges of Christianity, but these things remain in the realm of dream stuff.

We saw earlier how the invasion of Europe by Arabs and Berbers from North Africa had "annexed" the Iberian peninsula to Africa. Gradually Spain and Portugal reconquered their territories, but the last Muslim stronghold did not surrender till 1492. Away to the east Constantinople, the eastern bastion of Christendom, fell to the Muslim Turk in 1453. The Muslim was with difficulty turned back from Vienna as late as 1683. Long before the whole peninsula had been reconquered from Islam, the Portuguese had been trying to find a way around Muslim power so as to trade directly with India. As usual with human motives, there was a confused mixture in their minds which included religion. Thanks to the success and power of Islam, the Iberian kingdoms had been born in a "crusader" atmosphere, and the Portuguese wanted to deliver a mighty blow at the Muslims and to link up with Christian allies outside Europe. The legend of a "Prester John" with a Christian kingdom somewhere way out there—we do not know whether it was in Nubia, Ethiopia, or Asia—lured them on.

Some of the Muslims who met the Portuguese as they came round Africa recognized their old enemies. One who met them in India asked what devil had brought them there.

The Christianity brought by the Portuguese, though in essence unchanged, differed in a number of ways from that which had reached Africa in the first wave in the first centuries. It was more distinctly Western, and its official language and ceremonial was Latin. It looked to Rome as its center and could expect support (and control) from the state. As the Protestant and Catholic reformations of the sixteenth and seventeenth centuries made themselves felt, the Christianity reaching Africa by the sea routes was of a highly organized and self-consciously missionary kind, sensitive to threats to the faith and to deviations. It is sometimes difficult to see the humble Jewish carpenter in whom God dwelt so as to be accessible to man, in the face of this magnificent Christ—young, strong, well-disciplined in suffering and victory—but he is there for those who have eyes to see beyond his friends.

It is not easy for us to appreciate the achievements of the Christians, European and African, on the African coast during the fifteenth to the eighteenth centuries. For one thing, we are bound to associate this work with the Portuguese, and immediately one's mind gets tangled up with modern Portuguese policy in Angola and Mozambique. It is, however, possible to say that in the fifteenth and sixteenth centuries, when Portugal was the leading power in African waters, the local African land authorities had to be treated with a fair amount of respect; also many Africans seem to have found something attractive in the Portuguese of those earlier days. One of the first groups to land in South Africa was greeted by the local people with a dance, and the commander sent for the trumpeters so as to reply in kind.

We have to remember that these were the centuries when Portuguese, Italian, and German missionaries humbly approached civilizations greater than their own. In South India, de Nobili learnt to be a Sanskrit scholar so as to bring Christianity to the Hindus; in North India, Jerome Xavier bowed low in the Moghul court; in China, Ricci and Adam Schall studied Confucianism so as to make their way in Peking. Perhaps the white man's arrogance developed later.

Another factor which greatly befogs every issue at this time is the establishment by nations which called themselves Christian of the slave trade to America. We shall take up this point in detail somewhat further on in the story. We may now turn to consider briefly the second wave of Christianity in Africa during these centuries. At most places where they traded or called, the Portuguese kept an eye open for the possibility of starting Christian work. Very early they made attempts in the Gambia and Sierra Leone areas. Ten years before Columbus "who, in 1492, sailed over the ocean blue," so Ghanaian school children will tell you, an African king called Caramansa· permitted the first Christian service to be held on the soil of Ghana. At Benin, which is in modern Nigeria, the Portuguese found a powerful and flourishing African kingdom. Portuguese records were claiming the baptism of members of the Benin royal family as early as 1491. Among the Benin bronzes we see some of the Portuguese visitors as well as some Africans portrayed with crosses on their chests.

The most impressive Christian achievement of those days was in the Congo kingdom. The Portuguese navigators reached the Congo mouth in 1484, and within six years Congolese people had visited Portugal and missionaries had arrived. Before long the African king and queen were baptized. Their son was consecrated a bishop in 1518. Christianity greatly prospered, and there were strong hopes of the emergence of a Christianity which was genuinely African and yet catholic, but the Europeans insisted on ruining the kingdom by the slave trade and interference in politics. Moreover, the resources of Christianity in Portugal were not really adequate to the world-wide task she had assumed.

Some Christian work was done in Angola, but it suffered from the same disadvantages as in the Congo kingdom. Beyond Angola, on the way around Africa the Portuguese did not show much interest till they reached the mouth of the Zambesi. Here they found the old-established Muslim civilization which Ibn Battuta had mentioned, based on the trade in gold up into the hinterland kingdom of Monomotapa (Mwenye Matapa?), as they called it. Father Gonzalo da Silveira of the Society of Jesus went up into this kingdom in 1560. He baptized members of the royal family and hundreds of others, but suffered martyrdom within a year. It is possible that lasting Christian work might have resulted, but the Portuguese made a permanent settlement in the Mozambique area and meddled in the civil wars which eventually caused the collapse of the kingdom. When later

Christians came up they found few traces of the earlier work, though some canoe songs on the lower Zambesi may recall the chanting of the Fathers.

Further up the coast of eastern Africa, the Portuguese sacked Kilwa in 1505. A monstrance made from the fine light yellow gold they captured is to be seen in Lisbon to this day. Apart from the looting, they left behind a few representatives of their power, and some Franciscan friars asked to be left there too. We do not know quite how the work went. A few discontented women from Kilwa deserted their husbands and tried to run away in the ships, so causing a good deal of embarrassment to the admiral in charge of the fleet. A few slaves were also converted.

Still further north we come to Mombasa, now in Kenya. The city is on an island, and even in Ibn Battuta's day, as we saw earlier, it was quite a flourishing port and a center of Muslim civilization. Mombasa put up a very lively resistance to the Portuguese over a great number of years, but it was sacked by them no less than three times. In between, there was some response to the work of the Christian missionaries who came. Augustinian friars seem to have been loved by a large number of the people, who, even if they did not desert Islam, still respected these holy men who lived in poverty and tried to help others.

There was also at Mombasa a branch of the Misericordia, an organization run by the church with some financial help from the government, to look after people in need, especially orphans. We hear that during the work at Mombasa a number of well-born people from the town became Christians, so that here at least the work was not confined just to slaves and discontented women. It is most interesting to hear the story of a certain Yusuf bin Hassan who also had the African name Chingulia. His father had been an important person and leader in Mombasa and had fled away to Rabai, where he was killed by the local people, who had been bribed by the Portuguese. The young Yusuf had been taken away to Goa, in India, and there brought up along Portuguese lines. He had learned a good deal about warfare and was an expert at laying and firing guns. He obtained permission from the Portuguese to return to Mombasa in about 1627 and continued to appear to be a good Christian, but in 1631 he was able to make his way into the fort, stab the commander, and take over. He had to flee from there, and was eventually killed in the Red Sea area in about 1638. The Portuguese built at Mombasa one of their finest forts in the high tradition of Renaissance humanism. Its ground plan outline, like that of a Dogon village, is that of a man. It is called, ironically enough, Fort Jesus, and its grim ruins still dominate the entrance to the town and harbor of Mombasa from the seaward side.

In 1696 the Omanis from South Arabia were called in by the local people against the Portuguese, and they besieged the fort. It held out for no less than thirty-three months. It is something of a commentary on the relationship between the Portuguese and the local people that toward the end, when most of the Portuguese were dead, the fort was held for them partly by African women and a certain Swahili gentleman. Somehow the Portuguese had earned some kind of respect there.

Further north they were befriended from the beginning at Malindi. It was at Malindi that Vasco da Gama was able to find a deep sea pilot. The rulers of Malindi remained very friendly with the Portuguese for a long time, and we have evidence that they were quite prepared to let Christians in Malindi continue the practice of their religion. We even hear of an attempt at dialogue. There was a certain Portuguese in a threadbare cassock whose ship called at Malindi on his way to India, and some of the great men of Malindi came out to the ship to greet the captain and to ask if they could help in any way with necessities for their journey to India. Seeing this man in his cassock, one of the Muslims said that he hoped things were going well with the Christians in the matter of religion, because his own people at Malindi were not really paying as much attention as they should to their religion. Unfortunately he got rather a fanatical answer back. The person he was speaking to was none other than St. Francis Xavier, and the year was 1542.

We come now to the Portuguese expeditions to Ethiopia. The Portuguese had long wanted to make contact with the Christian Emperor in Ethiopia, and in 1487 they had sent a certain Pedro de Covilham by land to find him. Pedro had made his way down the East African coast and then finally overland to the Emperor. The Ethiopians, however, did not allow him to depart, and when some fellow countrymen came up later they found him married and settled down in the country. The sea expedition did in the end find its way round Africa, and after some years the Portuguese landed on the Red Sea coast and made their way up to the Emperor. An expedition of 1520 had as its chaplain a man called Francisco Alvarez, who has left a description of his visit. Francisco found that Lebna Dengel, who was now king, was a powerful ruler and did not need help from outside. He was involved in a large number of wars, so the Portuguese were able to go up and down the country and see how things were managed by the Ethiopians. In fact the expedition stayed there for no less than six years. While they were there, as was mentioned above, some Nubian Christians came asking for help.

After this expedition had left, the Muslims of the Red Sea coast area became aggressive. The king of Adal began to organize the attack on the Ethiopians, and his armies became more and more successful. Ahmed Ibn Ibrahim al Ghazi showed himself a most gifted leader. He was a left-handed man and had the surname of Gran. He harried the Ethiopian Emperor and his court and followers from one place to another, capturing stragglers and a good deal of treasure.

The Ethiopians appealed to the Portuguese, and at last in 1541 a Portuguese expedition of about four hundred men with firearms landed. The commander was Christopher da Gama, Vasco's relative. By this time Lebna Dengel was dead and Galawdewos (Claudius) was Emperor.

Gran had, by now, received reinforcements which included some "Turkish" gunmen. Portuguese and "Turks," Ethiopians and the followers of Ahmed Gran, met in many engagements, and then under the skillful leadership of Gran the Christian forces were defeated. Christopher was captured and, together with half the Portuguese, killed. The remaining Christian forces were put to rout. Local legend says it so happened that a Portuguese chemist escaped. With the help of the local people he made more gunpowder. The Ethiopian and Portuguese forces rallied and surprised Gran feasting in his camp, killed him, and put the Muslims to flight. More fighting with the Muslims followed, and even after that the Ethiopian Christians had to find some means of getting rid of the Portuguese.

The Portuguese wanted political power in return for the help they had given, and their church representatives also wanted the church of Ethiopia to "reform" itself in many of the things that seemed strange to them as Western Christians. They wanted them to come into line with the Western church in matters of doctrine and to accept the headship of His Holiness the Pope. This the Ethiopians were not prepared to do, and in due course they turned the priests out of their country. Having survived in their mountains for so long against so many enemies, they are naturally xenophobic. The adventures of Mussolini and his ecclesiastical supporters did little to reassure them. The Ethiopian church has emerged into the present day triumphantly unreformed, unwesternized, anti-Muslim, and conservative. Some who know and love her well say she needs her Henry VIII. Perhaps she will get her Stalin. If so, no doubt she will be as indestructible as the Russian church.

The glorious adventure of circumnavigating Africa and bringing together East and West had been entrusted to men unworthy of so high a calling. That day in 1498 when Vasco sailed into Calicut did not bring a new beginning in human relationships, but a tedious repetition of the old ugly cycle of war, exploitation, and then recrimination and revival. So also the bringing of a revived Christianity to Africa and Asia might have led to beautiful new things—but a religion cannot easily rise above the level of the people God has chosen to be its carriers.

CHAPTER THREE

The Lull and the Heroic Age

1. THE SLAVE TRADE

From the seventeenth to the nineteenth centuries things were quiet for both Christianity and Islam in Africa. The terrible pall of the slave trade lay over both religions, for "Christian" Spain, Portugal, France, Britain, Brandenburg, and Denmark, as well as "Muslim" Arabia, Persia, Iraq, Syria, Egypt, the Maghrib, and Turkey were all using Black Africa as a never-failing reservoir from which cheap labor could be drawn to run mines, fields, transport, harems, and armies. Christianity was born into a Judaism which accepted with disapprobation the fact of slavery as existing from time immemorial. Judaism looked upon the enslavement of its own members with great disfavor and laid down rules for a jubilee when they were to be freed. As Christianity moved into the Greco-Roman world it had to face slavery as a fact of society, but it always implied that it was an affront to God and would have to be done away with. In fact it worked for abolition in the Roman Empire, and in medieval Europe slavery did not exist as such, though in many respects feudal serfdom was not unlike it, and the fair-haired northerners sold "Slavs" to Muslims.

When, in the sixteenth century, a large-scale trade in slaves from

Africa began, it is clear that Christians realized they were doing wrong to take part in it. Catholic scholars can cite papal pronouncement after pronouncement against it. Equally on the Protestant side people knew it was wrong, but took centuries to do anything about it. The Quakers of Germantown in Pennsylvania in 1688 came out strongly against slavery—"those who steal or rob men and those who buy or purchase them, are they not all alike?"

John Newton, who in later life was a rector and wrote the hymn, "How sweet the name of Jesus sounds," was a slave-trader in his youth. His diary has come down to us as well as his testimony before Parliament. His life at sea was a hell, and for some time he himself became the virtual chattel of his master's black mistress on the West African coast. Sailors died like flies and tried to escape, but inexorably had to go on with their ghastly task, which, if profitable to someone, was not much good to those who did the work. The effect on Africa is not difficult to imagine, though the scale of devastation exceeds the grasp of our intellects. The white man did not catch his own slaves; his needs were met by African middlemen to whom he sold guns, firewater, and trinkets. They were coastal peoples who specialized in this work and went upcountry to capture or buy slaves. Slavery of various kinds had been known to African Traditional Religion and society; now wars for capturing slaves and the ordering of slaves into captivity by kings and chiefs became a commonplace.

To consider the effect on the mind of a human being captured in Africa and sold in the Americas after a voyage with which no inferno can compare, into a perpetual slavery into which his children would be born, makes the walls of one's own mind wobble with shock, yet by some miracle many Africans came through the experience with a dignity that puts their captors to shame. One of the first pieces of English literature written by an African is the account of his life by Olaudah Equiano or Gustavus Vassa the African, published in 1789. He was born around 1745 somewhere near Onitsha in eastern Nigeria. His mother tongue was Ibo. He was captured at the age of ten by African slavers who sent him down the river, where others sold him to white men who took him to the West Indies. By the time he was twenty-one, despite the treachery and cruelty he experienced from some, he had received help and encouragement from others and gained his freedom.

He served in Britain's wars in Canada and the Mediterranean and sailed as far as the Arctic. He had a deep Christian conversion experience and joined with the evangelicals and Quakers in their efforts to end the slave trade. He was well received by Christian groups in England and married an Englishwoman. He yearned to return to Africa as a missionary, but had to admit that his work lay in enlightening Europe. He died in 1797. His book was a best-seller in its day and still makes gripping reading, for it is brilliantly written.

For an account of the same kind of experiences at the hand of Muslim slave-traders we may refer to an account by another African author. The Mbotela family now lives near Mombasa in Kenya, and in the 1930's James Mbotela wrote in Swahili the story of the original member of the family, who was enslaved in the nineteenth century. He was a Yao living up in the region where the Ruvuma River goes toward Lake Nyasa. The Yao had been great continental traders and warriors. When in 1840 Sultan Seyyid Said moved his capital to Zanzibar, Arab and Swahili caravans began to penetrate to the great lakes of Central Africa, financed by Indian merchants from Gujerat. The Yao and other such tribes were given firearms, and they joined with the Swahili and Arabs in raids. They would surround a village, shoot fire arrows into the thatch, and capture people as they ran out. When villages began to concentrate and build *bomas* (thorn fences), slave trading became highly organized and decimated the population in areas which did not have strong central militarized governments. The area around Lake Nyasa (later Malawi), or west of Lake Tanganyika (later eastern Congo), suffered immensely. On the other hand, close-knit kingdoms such as Buganda underwent relatively little; Omukama Kabarega of Bunyoro (on the Nile between Lake Albert and Lake Kioga) beat off attack after attack of Egyptian slavers coming from Khartoum.

Mbotela remembered his early life in his home village in Yaoland: everything was perfect, everything bigger and better there and then than it was here and now. As a child he went catching flying ants when the termites swarmed, and herded goats. It was on one of these expeditions with a few other children that he was kidnaped by some Makua tribesmen who worked for a Swahili slaver. He was yoked with a stick to the next child and driven off by forced marches, beaten, hungry, and thirsty. Soon they came upon a group of bedraggled men and women who had been captured elsewhere. They, too, were yoked with slave sticks, and the drive towards the coast began. Some of the women had babes at the breast and they suffered greatly. One slaver deliberately killed a baby whose mother was lagging and reassured her that she would have many more children, the progeny of her masters.

On the way they became involved in an elephant hunt, because bringing slaves to the coast did not pay as well as using the slaves to transport ivory. They endured agonies as they were herded hither and thither during the elephant hunt and through a forest full of lions and other wild beasts. Those who complained or dragged their feet were clubbed to death, those who fell sick were left to die, and could see the hyenas and vultures gathering to eat them as their eyes closed in death.

At last they reached the Indian Ocean and were packed aboard a *dhow* as men pack dried fish. The boat slipped out to make the crossing to Zanzibar slave market, but was overtaken by a British man-of-war. In those days the Queen's Navy was still using sails, but some of the ships had engines as well. A captain had to conserve his coal, and if he failed to make a capture he had to pay for the coal himself. The Navy crews were often ill and terribly tired of the long, often fruitless cruises, but when they managed to capture a slave *dhow* they forgot their boredom in rushing to bring the slaves on deck and carry them to freedom. Often the slaves were frightened to death; they had suffered so much and had never seen such strange men and ships. The next problem was what to do with them. They could not just be dumped on the shores of Africa, where they would die or be reenslaved. The Navy brought them to Mombasa under frowning old Fort Jesus, falling into ruins since Portuguese days, and the missionaries resettled them at nearby Freretown.

Mbotela gradually grew used to his new life, but though he tried to study, and cultivated the piece of land he had been given, he still longed for home. The missionaries found him a wife; she was a Mnyasa, a weaker tribe the Yao had often raided, but now they were able to forget the enmities of the past.

Mbotela found the work he wanted when he became a gunbearer for explorers, traders, and missionaries going upcountry. He went on the expedition in which Bishop Hannington tried to enter Buganda by the back door and was speared to death in Busoga by the orders of the Kabaka. One wonders why Africans went on such expeditions, for the dangers were great, the pay small, and all the credit went to the European leading the expedition. Perhaps it was because they believed that they had a part to play in opening up the continent. Mbotela went many a long mile with "Bwana Dick," a European trader who was trying to establish trade routes across Maasai country. He finally died in a Maasai ambush trying to save Bwana Dick's life. The missionaries sent his son to England for education. Though his widow and children suffered much, the Mbotela family are today among Kenya's leading families.

In discussing the dual culpability of Christians and Muslims in the African slave trade, our discussion group in the University of Ghana noted the hypocrisy of leading Christian missionaries and churchmen in the latter nineteenth century, in whipping up support for "Christian" crusades against "Muslim" slave raiding in the Niger area, the Sudan, Malawi, and the Congo, when less than a century earlier their countrymen had been doing it themselves. Muslims remarked that it was typical of Christian idealism that at a high level it condemned slavery out of hand, while the thing itself continued to exist for another few centuries and in a form more pernicious than the world had ever seen before. (Just like the basic Christian refusal to admit the possibility of divorce, while ever crazier divorce laws are enacted all over the West.) Islam was much more practical. It accepted men for what they were and did everything it could to alleviate the suffering of the slaves and bring about their emancipation.

We all agreed that Islam as such and Christianity as such can hardly be blamed for the wickedness of individual members, but none of us could find a quick answer for the African student who, taking a Marxist line, said that Christianity, Islam, and African Traditional Religion for that matter, were all aiders and abettors of the slave trade for economic and social reasons, and this just proved what nonsense religion is. In such a general failure of religion and common humanity, even if one did not know of one already, a person would be tempted to hope there is a God who can provide some means of covering and expiating so crushing a weight of man-made evil.

2. THE ERA OF THE CHAPLAINS

From about 1517 onward Western Christianity has been openly divided. On the Catholic side we saw how Portuguese efforts in Africa declined. Spain had enough to occupy her church's attention in the Americas and the Philippines. France eliminated her Protestants in 1685 and tried to promote Catholic Christianity in various parts of the world, but her main interests lay in Canada, the West Indies, and India—not as yet in Africa. Fortunately, in 1622 the Holy See had reorganizcd the central Roman direction of missions under the College of Propaganda, so that some help could be organized for Christians in Africa.

Perhaps the story of the Christians at Ouidah (Whydah) in Dahomey will illustrate the kind of ups and downs suffered by Christians on the coast of Africa at that time. The Portuguese gathered a congregation there which lived on after the decline of their power. Passing French priests helped when they could, and some French Capuchins came in the middle of the seventeenth century. They were followed by a Belgian Capuchin. After this, priests from Fernando Po visited occasionally. In the late eighteenth century, slaves who had obtained their release in Brazil began to come back. Many were pious Catholics (some were Muslim), and in due course in the nineteenth century the Catholic church as well as the Wesleyans made Ouidah a base for expansion inland.

On the Protestant side, the Dutch East India Company tried to find chaplaincy help for its own employees, but for the rest tended to adapt its religious policy to whatever paid best dividends. (The English East India Company had an even more disgraceful policy but does not enter our story here.) When the Dutch took Elmina in 1637 they called a halt to Catholic work, but found sooner or later that they had to organize something of a school. The most famous teacher at this school was Elisa Johannes Capitein, who was sent as a young boy to Holland and educated there. He graduated at Leyden University and was ordained as a minister of the Dutch Reformed Church. Coming back to Elmina in 1742, he began the work of translating the Lord's Prayer, the Commandments, and various articles of faith into the local language. The trouble that overtakes other chaplains caught up with him: he was working in a secular atmosphere on a small and intermittent salary, so became involved in trade and gradually drifted out of chaplaincy work. He died in 1747, but he had achieved something.

In South Africa, as we shall see, Dutch work was on a broader basis.

The English reformed their church in the sixteenth century and claimed it was a continuation of the ancient church of the primitive fathers and of their own land. When they dissolved the monasteries and religious orders, they lost some of the chief traditional means of propagating the faith overseas, though many Anglicans would claim to this day that the apostolic method is to appoint bishops and clergy to this task. In 1701, using the contemporary method of setting up a company by royal charter, they established the Society for the Propagation of the Gospel, which sent chaplains to the American colonies and to African forts such as Cape Coast in Ghana. One of these, Thomas Thompson, sent a young African called Philip Quaque to England in 1764. There he received a good education and married an English girl. He returned home and ran a school for children connected with the fort and a number of other Africans who were interested. He, too, had to trade to finance himself. A leading Ghanaian educationalist has said that schools like this were the basis on which modern education in Ghana was built.

At Christiansborg (Osu), the Danish colony near Accra, was the little school where Christian Protten, son of a Danish father and a Ga mother, studied. He was sent to Denmark and there came under the influence of the Moravian Brethren, who sent him and a number of other people back to the coast, which was still the "white man's grave"; Europeans sent to work there soon died of malaria, yellow fever, or dysentery.

Christian resources were meager and cultural or other contact between the Christians and non-Christians slight; the main preoccupation of many people who might have been concerned was trade and how to get home before entering the grave. One of the deadly side effects of the slave trade was to paralyze other forms of contact and interchange. It is remarkable that anything at all was achieved.

3. THE CHRISTIAN REVIVAL

From 1789 to 1815 Europe was convulsed by one of those civil wars which brought her (and in the end the world) to the brink of catastrophe. During this time various Christians, including the evangelical party in the Church of England, were able to lobby enough support to get Parliament to declare the slave trade illegal in 1808. Britain had been the main operator in it during the previous century or so, and now she used all her power to bring it to an end. Former criminals often make good police. The real heroes here were the riffraff of the 'fore-the-mast-men who bore the hardships of the patrols in tropical waters.

A religious revival was gripping the Western world. The work of Wesley had its effect in Europe and America and was itself interlinked with that of the Moravian Brethren and the Pietists in Germany. The Protestants had discovered their missionary vocation and began to found societies "to send out men to preach the gospel to every nation." In Catholic Europe, after the sufferings undergone by the church and the papacy at the hands of revolutionaries, a more vigorous, organized, and militant form of faith emerged.

On the other side of the affair, the Africans were, as always, ready to receive people who came to them peacefully and with good intentions. Few other countries have been so hospitable to strangers. So from the end of the Napoleonic wars till the mid-1880's, when colonial fever overcame the Europeans, there was a kind of heroic age when Christians came into various parts of Africa to preach, and Africans responded and took on the work. There were fewer extraneous factors like the slave trade and colonialism to cloud the main issues. The hour called for great men as individuals and in groups, and they were forthcoming. It is not easy to outline their story at all adequately. It would be simplest perhaps to give their biographies, yet their stories merge and blur with the story of the churches they founded and served, and these themselves flow into the stories of the African countries concerned. Let us glance at a few.

The church in Sierra Leone was started before the French Revolution by the bringing in of people of African ancestry who had become Christians elsewhere. These included black Nova Scotians who had taken the British side in the American independence movement, and maroons (militant runaway slaves) from Jamaica. The United States took a great deal of interest in the *"Amistad* case." According to local oral tradition, this slave ship was going from one Cuban port to another when, in 1839, the slaves threw most of their captors overboard and told the two surviving Spaniards to navigate them back to Africa. Instead, they took them northward into U.S. waters and were taken into port by the authorities. A clever professor from Yale suggested that the Blacks count in their own language, until someone recognized the language: the men were Mende from Sierra Leone. After a long lawsuit they were vindicated and sent back home, together with some Americans who wanted to work in their country. This support has not ceased.

When the British Navy began to intercept slave ships, the freed men were landed in Sierra Leone. The Church Missionary Society, founded in 1799 by a group of British evangelicals with the kind of parliamentary and chartered company organization they understood, began to send help. Other religious bodies also assisted. The liberated slaves were settled in villages and the colony divided up into parishes, for each of which a minister was provided. It was more and more necessary to give the people means of employment and education. Bell's system of education, by which children taught one another with the aid of pupil-teachers, which had been tried out in Madras (where it educated the writer's mother and grandmother), was in 1817 brought to Sierra Leone. We have to remember that education in Britain at this time was not well developed, and people who criticize the work of the missions in Africa as regards education forget that quite often in Africa facilities were better than in the missionaries' home countries. One notable example of this is the work of Fourah Bay College, which was founded in 1827. Its main purpose was to train teachers and ministers of religion, some of whom studied Hebrew and Arabic. The college went through many ups and downs and times of severe financial neglect and shortage before growing into the university it now is. Nevertheless, for a good part of its career it has been a great academic institution.

Higher education for girls was also started in Sierra Leone at the delightfully named Female Institution, in 1845. Thus by the middle of the century there was present the whole apparatus for primary, secondary, and higher education for both boys and girls. A great deal of language work was done by the missionaries in Sierra Leone. There were a number of people like Hannah Kilham of the Society of Friends, who insisted that people would never understand the Christian message if it came to them through the medium of a foreign language. Koelle, the German missionary sent by the Church Missionary Society, was a most capable linguist, and his *Polyglotta Africana,* which brings together words from a number of different African languages which the good scholar collected from freed slaves, has remained a monument of the linguistic work done by so many of the missionaries in Africa.

Sierra Leoneans love to criticize themselves, and it is most interesting to get them to debate the question whether the Christian effort in Sierra Leone met the high hopes that had been placed in it. People had supposed that Sierra Leone would become the light in the darkness from which Christianity would radiate in every direction. There have been bitter disappointments and failures. Yet there were some remarkable adventures. Thus some Sierra Leonean released slaves bought an old slave ship and used it to ply up and down the coast to Lagos to trade and to preach. It was also Sierra Leoneans who played an important part in the mission to Yorubaland and up the Niger.

The churches in Liberia were started in the 1820's by "free people of color" sent back by various American societies and groups. These colonists, who were themselves ex-slaves or descended from black Americans who had gained their freedom, were of many different denominations—Baptist, Methodist, Presbyterian, Episcopal, Catholic, Quaker and so on. Over the years they obtained all too little support from the mission bodies related to their churches, and struggled on against many difficulties. A person studying the history of Christianity in Liberia finds the story of a struggle for survival, with a fair measure of sorrow and disappointment, yet it was from here that two men of the utmost importance to African Christianity came.

Edward Wilmot Blyden was born in 1832 in the then Danish West Indian Island of St. Thomas. He migrated to Liberia in 1851. He was one of the most learned men of his time, and he carefully studied Arabic and paid great attention to indigenous African civilization, as well as being a scholar in the Western classics. He was himself an ordained minister and knew his Christianity thoroughly. At the same time he could appreciate Islam. It is not complimentary to Blyden, Christianity, Islam, or Africans to imply as some people do in discussion that he looked upon Islam as a form of higher religion to which Africans could attain more easily than to Christianity. Rather he used Islam as a mirror to hold up before bad Christians: he showed how it could unify men in the face of racism, how it produced educated men and civilization based on highly developed commerce and industry. In some ways it would be natural for an African to move toward this religion and civilization rather than toward one carried by Westerners who had themselves drifted away from the basic virtues of their faith. His was an appeal for better Christianity rather than more Islam —though he was a big enough Christian to rejoice in the prosperity of a sister religion. After suffering a number of personal insults (he lost one appointment because of the rumor that he had gone to bed with the President's wife) and being made the victim of various underhand dealings, Dr. Blyden began to call upon African Christians to secede from the churches dominated by people who were stifling the work of God's Holy Spirit. Remarkably enough, this challenge met with comparatively little response. The members of the main stream of West African Christianity patiently went on working with their white brothers and waited over half a century, taking over their independence stage by stage. History allows us no "but if only's," yet it is true that too much patience can quench the Spirit.

The second man, William Wadé Harris, was one of the group labeled in those days "Kroomen," a member of the Grebo people. He was born around 1850 and attended an American Methodist school and himself taught in an American Episcopal school. He joined in some rioting and in prison had a vision. At about the age of sixty he went off preaching and baptizing into the neighboring Ivory Coast and onward toward Gold Coast/Ghana. He told people to destroy their former objects of worship and turn to the one true God and the Savior he sent to die upon the Cross. Tens of thousands answered his call until 1915, when the French colonial governor quietly pushed him back over the border. After some years missionaries, mainly Methodist and Catholic, followed up his work. A vigorous *église harriste* also exists.

Something must be said about two pioneer churches in Gold Coast/Ghana. Some of the African and Afro-European young men educated at the little school at Cape Coast formed a "Bible Band" for Bible study and general education. Their request for help eventually reached the Wesleyan Mission Society, who sent out a group in 1835. These and their successors were all fairly promptly in their graves, till Thomas Birch Freeman arrived in 1838. This was an Englishman whose father was a Black, perhaps one of those slaves who had been declared free in the century before by the judgment of Lord Mansfield that no one on English soil could be accounted a slave. T.B.F. (as Ghanaian students call him) had a good education and the usual Victorian knack of self-betterment. He had been trained as a gardener and had taught himself botany. He also had the gift of bringing out local resources and cooperation. Though other forms of Christianity have flourished in the area, a special relationship grew up between the Fante people and Methodism. Fante canoemen carried Christianity down the coast, and Fante traders head-loaded it up into the forest. They took happily to Methodist organization in committees and class meetings; readily kept minutes, recognized precedents, and voted accepting personal defeat by vote while supporting the policy which won the general vote of the committee or group. A Ghanaian politician has said that the basic organization of democratic and civil service method was learned in Christian groups such as these.

Freeman himself made epic missionary journeys to visit the king of Ashanti and King Gezo in Dahomey. He started Methodist work in Yorubaland. He was a man of apostolic stature and he thought big. One year he spent more for the church than the local British representative in charge of the Gold Coast forts had at his disposal. As with many other apostolic men, his accounts could face God but not an accountant. He had to retire from the ministry for a while, but returned to full-time service long before he died in 1890.

On the east central coast of Gold Coast/Ghana, men and women sent by the Basel Mission from 1828 onward used Christiansborg (Osu), the Danish fort, as their place of landing. Andreas Riis, from Schleswig-Holstein, broke through the coastal curtain with some African friends and set up an inland base at Akropong with the consent of the African king (and no doubt queen) and "nation." He brought in West Indian Blacks to help him. The Twi-speaking people of the Akwapim ridge country and the Ga-speaking people of the plain behind Accra joined in heartily after some initial setbacks. This group, European and African, did some superb language work, taught craftsmanship, self-improvement, and better agriculture and marketing. In the fullness of time men and women went into the rest of the country speaking impeccable Twi, with a Bible in one hand and a cocoa plant in the other.

In the area we today refer to as southwestern Nigeria and southeastern Dahomey, in the nineteenth century the Yoruba people faced a whole series of civil wars as well as invasions by the Dahomean armies in the southwest and Fulani forces in the northeast. In 1851 the British captured a base at Lagos, and the French at times exercised some power off parts of the coast; but beyond the reach of these sea-based guns the Yoruba themselves were in authority. Thus, when missionaries came up in the 1840's sent by various British or French or American societies, they had to wait on the local ruler to get permission to start work. The latter had to consult every section of his community and in the meantime accommodate and feed the wretched visitors. Then the missionaries would be given or leased some land at a nominal rental, and closely watched for some time. They could do little until they had learned the language and until some person who knew the local etiquette and society joined in to help them. These helpers were nearly always "marginal" men—perhaps bright young men who found African gerontocracy tedious—and were often taken into the missionaries' homes and dubbed "houseboys." The white-robed army of houseboys has provided martyrs, saints, and even prime ministers. The first converts were often men who had traveled and returned. The greatest of these was Samuel Adjai Crowther. He was captured in a Yoruba war, and after passing through the hands of various African masters, was sold to a Portuguese who shipped him for the trans-Atlantic crossing. The British intercepted the ship at sea and landed its cargo at Sierra Leone. Here the young Adjai received an education better than many people in Britain or the United States could obtain in those days. He took part in the ill-fated expedition up the Niger in 1841, when a great number of the people on the ship died of fever—a failure which dashed the aspirations of philanthropists who had hoped to bring Christianity and honest commerce to inland Africa. He was among the first missionaries into Yorubaland, and was preaching there one day when his mother, standing among the listeners, recognized her long-lost son who had, as it were, reappeared from the dead.

In Britain itself he was always well-received and given the honor his achievements deserved. Prince Albert learnt much about Africa from him, and Crowther noticed that he called the attentive lady in the background "Your Majesty"—none other than the great Queen. Oxford recognized his language work with a doctorate. He was consecrated bishop and returned to lead the mission up the Niger.

The adventures of the great Crowther for many years galvanized the Victorian Christian public. Once he was kidnaped, and a young Englishman came to rescue him: they dashed for the boat together but the young man stopped an arrow, dying happy that he had done his duty. Another time Crowther suffered shipwreck in the rapids and walked back hundreds of miles overland, preaching and planning as he went.

At Calabar to the east of the Niger mouth, Scots missionaries like the intrepid Mary Slessor and the local people who had been in contact with the outside world for centuries had done some intensive pioneer work, but there had been little penetration of the river. In a surprisingly few years, with ludicrously small resources, the black bishop established Christian centers where a church and school were set up under the direction of an African teacher. Quite often these men were Sierra Leoneans or West Coast Africans. The financial rewards were minimal compared with their responsibilities and the economic potentialities of their positions. Often a teacher's wife with the West African woman's genius for trade and marketing could make more money than her husband. Crowther, in the best apostolic tradition, was prepared to let local resources be used and to let things develop naturally. He began to push up beyond the Niger-Benue confluence towards the Muslim lands of the north: the work there had great promise.

Late in Bishop Crowther's ministry the colonial fever had begun to grip many Europeans. It would be surprising if members of mission boards and societies did not begin to sneeze in such an epidemic. Henry Venn, who had been general secretary to the Church Missionary Society until 1872, and who had been greatly influenced by Rufus Anderson, secretary of the American board, had consistently supported the idea of African missions run by Africans. Now some of the board members and younger missionaries began to insist that things should be more centrally organized and administered and that they should play a more important part. Various inquiries were instituted, but nothing substantial could be proved against the Bishop's helpers; the old man died in 1891 in great sorrow. A schism of crippling proportions was only prevented by the seemingly limitless patience of the majority of the African church people. The church in Nigeria had entered the colonial period.

In East Africa there may have been some Christians before the nineteenth century. Excavations show there were Christians in medieval times on the island of Socotra, in the Indian ocean off the horn of Africa. The various Indian and other sailors down the coast may well have included Christians, but no definite findings have yet been unearthed. So the credit for bringing Christianity goes to Ludwig Krapf, a German trained at Basel who was working for the Church Missionary Society. He reached Mombasa in 1844, and the first service he conducted was the funeral of his wife and infant daughter. He wrote soon afterward about stepping over their graves to the evangelization of Africa. To people looking to count how many converts were made, he would appear to have accomplished little. But he saw Mount Kenya with her eternal snows upon the equator, and laid the foundation for the study of Swahili, a language which has a great literature and a long future. To put it in Victorian idiom, he rescued it from being a Muslim language. Like David Livingstone, he made close friendships with Africans and refused to shoot his way out of tight situations. When his Kamba friend Kivoi was killed, he did not fire, but afterward found the barrel of his gun useful for carrying water. When he lay dying he quoted the French Imperial Guard at Waterloo: "The Guard does not surrender, it dies."

Krapf's work was followed up by others, including Charles New, who brought Methodist support. The Holy Ghost Fathers came to Zanzibar in 1863 and went on to Bagamoyo in 1868, but even so, Christianity in Kenya and Tanzania had to wait a long time for any large-scale achievement. The spectacular break-through in East Africa came eight hundred miles inland by the great lakes of Uganda.

The story is well-known. In 1875 Stanley, the Anglo-American explorer, visited Buganda. This was a powerful, highly cultured and organized kingdom centered round the Kabaka, who seemed to hold absolute sway over spirits and men. (No individual traditional ruler can be absolute in his own person, though outsiders may see him as such.) The traditional beliefs, culture, and society were strong and intact; they were closely intertwined—in fact, the Ganda system was strong not only then, but survived into the modern world, and those who have had dealings with it know its subtlety, resilience, and stubborn self-confidence. As we shall see, Muslim traders from the east coast had reached Buganda many years before, and Islam was about to experience a fearful persecution.

Kabaka Mutesa received Stanley well and showed great interest in Christianity. Perhaps it was the power that "Christians" like Stanley had—firearms especially—that fascinated him most. Also it is part of Ganda courtesy that when one is in a relaxed mood one dwells on subjects which please one's guest. Stanley, nicknamed the "Breaker of Rocks," brutal, tough, and ruthless, who had the stern background of a Welsh poorhouse and the hurly-burly of American journalism behind him, liked to go religious at such times. He thought Christianity would do good in Buganda, and he felt Buganda would be a feather in Christianity's cap. The Kabaka gave the explorer the impression that he would like missionaries, and Stanley sent a message to the London *Daily Telegraph.*

It was two years before the Church Missionary Society of the Church of England managed to send a group of men, who arrived in June 1877. In 1879 a party of White Fathers sent by Cardinal Lavigerie's society based on France and Algiers, with full backing from Rome, arrived in Entebbe. There is a saying among the pious that Christ was born crucified. Certainly in Africa his body, the church, was born divided. Both parties denounced Islam; Mackay, the dour Scot of the "English" group told the Kabaka some of his views on Catholics, their pope, and their devotion to the Blessed Virgin; Père Lourdel on his side believed there was one true church, his own, so that the Anglicans having got there first meant nothing—the true faith had to be proclaimed. Fortunately there was plenty of room for everybody; both sides included men of apostolic greatness and God's good news was preached. In Buganda everything that mattered happened at the Kabaka's court. There were the chiefs who administered the country under the Kabaka and there were the young men, "the pages," who would succeed them. Day by day the missionaries taught, and the most important people in the kingdom heard them. The

Kabaka himself assisted with the work.

Kabaka Mutesa was one of the cleverest statesmen of the nineteenth century. His son Mwanga was not so secure amidst the various elements of the internal power structure of Ganda politics, quite apart from the strains imposed by the presence of two sects of missionaries who had the leading imperialist powers of the day behind them. It was the decade of the "scramble for Africa." In 1886 Mwanga turned to persecution, and before long the young church (Roman Catholic and Anglican) was crowned with a glorious company of martyrs of which any church could be proud. We do not know exactly what went on in the Kabaka's mind. Kagwa and other Ganda writers say Arabs had introduced homosexual practices and that the Kabaka was enraged when young men and boys who had become Christian refused to join in. This is to attribute too much to the Arabs, for it is most unlikely that any human society does not know of these things, though Victorian missionaries and their followers with their "noble savage" and "Oriental depravity" attitudes would have us think so. More probably the Kabaka felt that the Christians had gone too far in pulling apart the Ganda way of life and would have to be brought to heel. Also it was pretty plain that among the high officials and executioners were many who thought the Christians should be repressed, swiftly, fiercely, and drastically.

It is a good deal easier for us to catch a glimmer of the minds of some of the young men who were martyred. In the collecting and sifting of evidence which is part of the Catholic process of beatification and canonization, a great deal of information about these young men is available. Probably they are among the best known of all young Africans who grew up in the premodern period. In them we may see mirrored the type of young African manhood which over the thousands of years which had gone before had conquered the continent and built up a great and civilized society. Calling on Christ, singing and cheerful, Catholics and Protestants in their scores, they went to their deaths; some to be strangled, some to be sawn asunder, some to be burned.

The young men who did not suffer martyrdom bided their time, learning all they could about Christianity and organizing for the future. In the civil wars that followed, the Catholics, the Protestants, and the Muslims overcame the traditionalists and clipped the wings of the Kabaka. Then they turned on one another: the Muslims were given the smallest prizes, the Catholics the next, and the Protestants took the biggest—by this time (1890–92) they had a white man with a Maxim gun to help. Allowing for what human beings of any nation will do with religion, in Uganda Christianity (both Catholic and Protestant) and an Islam of the finest quality rooted themselves in the African soil. More will be said later about this country which both Dr. Billy Graham and His Holiness Pope Paul have considered the most Christian in Africa.

We turn briefly now to South Africa. To the long-haul East Indiamen, southern Europe and Africa were obstacles on the way to the East. It was not until 1652 that a few Dutchmen were put ashore at the Cape of Good Hope to ensure the supply of fresh meat and vegetables and water for the passing ships. Gradually this grew into a settlement and colonists began to arrive: Huguenots, for instance, French Protestants fleeing from persecution, came in the 1680's. The local inhabitants were Bushmen away toward the north and west. They lived their own amazing life of survival and do not enter our picture at this time. Then there were the so-called Hottentots, a hunting and gathering people with some cattle. Considering the fate of California Indians, it is a miracle that they survived. (In Johannesburg it is whispered that they not only survive, but that there is Hottentot blood in many of the strongest advocates of *apartheid.*) Then coming in from the northeast were the "Bantu," which include such peoples as the Zulu and Xhosa.

In 1737 Georg Schmidt of the Moravian Brethren started work among the Hottentots, but he met with a great deal of suspicion from the local Dutch Reformed Church, which denied his right to baptize. He left, a disappointed man, but when the Brethren returned in 1792 they found some of Schmidt's work had survived. They adopted the idea of taking their people apart into self-contained settlements or communes, there to Christianize them and prepare them to exist in this modern, wicked world. Many other groups have used the same concept, and perhaps it is necessary at a certain stage in the work, but it tends to linger long after it has become dangerous.

The young London Missionary Society (founded 1795 as an interdenominational body which became increasingly Congregationalist) sent Dr. Vanderkemp, a Dutch ex-soldier and physician, to South

Africa in 1799. He set up a refuge for Hottentots and tried to protect them from the settlers who wanted them to settle on their farms and work. Vanderkemp married a freed Malagasy slave and in various other ways scandalized the dominant society. The London Missionary Society sent John Philip in 1821, and he too managed in his own way to keep the tradition of being a nuisance. He agitated for the rights of "persons of color" and insisted that the African chiefs on the frontier should be treated not as cattle-raiders but as political leaders whose territories were being encroached on. He begged his fellow Christians not to treat the Hottentots as perpetual wards of the church. In 1840 David Livingstone, another London Missionary Society man, went upcountry to Kuruman. The Boers had to treat him severely because he insisted on saying that their use of African labor was no better than slave-owning, and he fraternized with Africans even to the extent of giving them guns as gifts.

His subsequent adventures deserve detailed study, but suffice it here to say that with the aid of African helpers and usually far from the protection of foreign guns, he was able to explore a great part of Africa as far as Tanzania and the Congo. In burning, self-sacrificing sincerity he thought he was opening up Africa for Christianity and (honest) commerce. African students agree that in the long run he did this, but they point out that his more immediate followers included folk like Cecil Rhodes and King Leopold.

South Africa became a kind of happy hunting ground for every denomination under the sun; at the same time nearly every device for missionary work was tried out there. (South Africa has an immense store of experience in religion, science, and agriculture under African conditions which was once available to all and may be so again. The writer, being of Indian origin, found it difficult to pursue his usual method of wandering round churches, mosques, libraries, and universities without being a potential embarrassment to his hosts, African and "white," even though they were willing enough. Academic journals and monographs published in South Africa often come under a general ban on South African goods in Black Africa.)

There is not time to say more than a few words about some of the religious groups and their work. The Scots as usual concentrated on education, industrial missions, and medicine, which at that time they were successfully bringing to England and America as well as Africa.

Their institutions at Lovedale and Fort Hare trained teachers, artisans, nurses, and ministers of religion as well as men who became leading politicians and educationalists in many parts of Africa.

The churches of the Dutch Reformed tradition (which some of the more impish Uganda students like to call "Deformed") in various forms—there is no need here to go into details about "Hervormde Kerk" and "Gereformeerde"—from fairly early days have tried a pattern of separate development for "whites" and "nonwhites." Its theologians have had a difficult task with the Old Testament stories about a Chosen People and their converse—a group under a curse. St. Paul explicitly put "racial" and cultural differences on the same basis as circumcision and uncircumcision. In the course of revelation to the Jews, the recognition of a difference may have been useful, but God had a plan for both. In Christ, Jew and Greek and barbarian are one. The "trekkers" who went out across the wilderness to a promised land flowing with milk and honey, who fought off the former inhabitants, etc., have remained a dominant white man's myth in South Africa. (In many parts of America it has its own local variation and applications.) Their church did not in the first place encourage the "trekkers," and their best theologians have reminded them that no human group can arrogate to itself the title of "Chosen People," especially if they do not live up to the vocation of love for all.

Roman Catholic work encountered difficulty in the early times because of the militant Protestantism of the Dutch of those days, but was able from the 1850's to begin work which in the last seventy years has expanded vastly. Their work and that of the Paris Mission in Basutoland (Lesotho) has created an African folk Christianity which is interesting to compare with similar phenomena among the Chagga of Tanzania and the Ganda.

Other important efforts can just be mentioned. Methodist work, based on the idea of dual congregations and chains of stations, has had a great response. The Anglican Province of South Africa has a fascinating history of African and British ideas merging and meeting and clashing with each other and the views of Africaans churchmen. Various German groups such as the Rhenish, Hermannsburg, and Berlin societies have left their mark. In 1835 South Africa was one of the first places to receive men sent overseas by the American Board of Commissioners for Foreign Missions. Soon they ran into the crossfire of the wars between the Boers and the Zulu and Matabele whom they had come to serve, but eventually were able to assist their African friends to find a means of building a new life after the failure of Chaka and Dingaan to use Zulu power to ensure unbroken corporate survival into the twentieth century. (The Zulu deserved this as much as the Ashanti and the Ganda.)

Like a cloud no bigger than a man's hand which was in the end to fill the sky, we discover the emergence of "separatist" churches in South Africa as early as 1872. There will be more to say of them later.

Christianity had spread apace and gone deep in the country long before Britain in her high imperialist mood of late Victorian days fully realized that South Africa was part of her empire, "on which the sun never set." Christianity at the southern end of the continent was the launching pad for a great deal of other missionary effort in the continent as a whole. The work of David Livingstone is the best known, but we ought not to be ignorant of the obscure Africans trained in South Africa who went out to teach and preach or give examples of Christian woman- and wifehood. We may take Bernard Mizeki as an example. He was born in Mozambique around the year 1861 and went to work in a "white" household in Cape Town. A young German lady befriended him and helped him to get an education. He went up into newly-formed Rhodesia and began work among the Shona as a teacher and evangelist. He was speared to death in 1896, dying, as his friends viewed it, for his Lord. Presumably from his killers' point of view he died for his association with Cecil Rhodes, who was a nonbeliever but found missions useful.

By this time in our proceedings somebody in the seminar was bound to point out that apparently the Catholics did not do much in Africa between the Napoleonic wars and the "scramble for Africa." "Apparently" is the operative word, mainly because the achievement of these years looks small as compared with the miracle they wrought between 1910 and 1960. The Catholic church on the human side (who would presume to speak of the divine?) is one of the oldest living human organizations and had a highly developed centralized bureaucracy when French, Germans, and English were barbaric savages and the Americans had not been thought of. Her scholars and exchangers of information act as a kind of memory or intelligence, experience gained in one country and one age can be applied in another ("Sometimes it takes half a century," remarked a young priest with a friendly groan). In the nineteenth century the church had some pretty massive internal problems of modernization to deal with in Italy and France, so she could not be rushed into changing missionary standards or methods overnight. The Protestants clearly had the initiative, the ball was at their feet (we shall see later whether it had a chain attached to it). The burgeoning Industrial Revolution gave these folk from northern Europe and eastern U.S.A. a leisured and monied class who had enthusiasm, ready cash, and personnel to spare for such quixotic adventures (Dickens, for one, could make much fun of them). The southern Irish, the southern Dutch, and various Catholic minorities in North America who later gave so much to Africa were still submerged.

The Protestants were not internationally and centrally based on fundamentally ecclesiastical structures and personnel. In Britain or Germany or the U.S.A. a group of laity could push ahead using secular ideas and methods with local support without needing to refer to anyone. They could make an artisan with no theological training the leader of an expedition, or send out a convert with little general knowledge or education as a preacher. The Catholics in the main insisted on sacerdotal leadership and would not tamper with the view that a Catholic priest is a Catholic priest wherever he comes from; his training must be thorough, and so far as possible include the same basic study. When people coming to Africa died like flies, this made missions a little difficult to conduct. The mission up on the Nile south of Khartoum, based on support from Verona, Italy, and Vienna, was not large numerically but lost seventy men in forty years from 1847 on. The Society for African Missions lost two hundred and eighty missionaries in West Africa in sixty-five years; the Holy Ghost Fathers in East and West Africa between 1843 and 1900 lost more than six hundred. Protestant losses were comparable—the Basel Mission lost ninety-one in fifty-eight years, the Church Missionary Society fifty-three in twenty years—but they were not so difficult to replace. A Kenyan girl student pointed out that the Protestant societies with no long history behind them could try new methods and find great use for the growing number of women of education and means who were not content to sit in comfortable withdrawing rooms gossiping and being pregnant. The Protestant lady-teacher and missionary wife (often carefully posted where she could supervise domestic affairs for her husband's bachelor colleagues as well) played an increasingly vital role in Africa. On the other side this is a difficult point to discuss, for the Catholic Church never lacked women's orders. It looks as if some considerable revamping of the rules for nuns, and increase in their numbers, had taken place by the end of our period, but for some time the vital woman-to-woman contact which is essential in the propagation of religion was stronger on the Protestant side.

The Catholics also seemed to choose what a Muslim colleague called the "stonier parts of their Lord's vineyard." Algeria and Tunisia swallowed up an incredible proportion of Catholic effort with little to show for it, even after 1867, when Lavigerie took over as archbishop. The Holy Ghost Fathers in East Africa in this period worked in Zanzibar and the mainland opposite. They did language work and assisted freed slaves and gained experience vital for the next stage, but Islam was already there in strength.

In West Africa a notable event was the sending of a certain Father Barron in 1841 by some of the American Catholic bishops to find out how their people were faring in Liberia. He went on to Rome to report and was made Vicar Apostolic of the Two Guineas. Proceeding to France for support, he was lucky enough to get in touch with the Society of the Sacred Heart recently founded by Francis Libermann, a convert from Judaism. He was given seven men. When Mgr. Barron reached Liberia he considered the position hopeless and returned home. Two of his men went to Senegal, where they tried to link up with the old established French Catholic work at Goree, in the Dakar area and St. Louis. This work however did not really begin to prosper till 1863, when Dakar became the center of a Vicariate Apostolic, and later when they could push inland beyond the Muslim zone.

Two of Mgr. Barron's men went to the Ivory Coast but had to turn back. One went to the Gabun river. This was Jean Remi Bessieux, who became a bishop and was able to continue the mission with the help of the Holy Ghost Fathers with whom Libermann's group had amalgamated in 1848.

By the end of the period under discussion, Cardinal Lavigerie's White Fathers had made a break-through in Uganda, and the Society for African Missions (S.M.A.) was about to do the same in Gold Coast/Ghana and Nigeria. It is not possible to gauge "success" in this kind of situation; the mere laying down of many lives or persistence in the face of "failure" may be success. The gaining of vast numbers may mean failure. The test of true Christian strength is to be able to face these two deceivers.

By this time in the nineteenth century (the 1880's), Christianity had begun to spring up in many vital African centers. The work was going ahead largely independent of foreign political control, and Africans were taking an increasing share. The promise for the future was great. At this point foreign political and economic intrusion took place on a scale and with a speed and depth no other continent has ever suffered. The colonial intervention overran the mission institutions, and it is the current historical myth that the colonial and imperial period brought Christianity a tremendous advantage. Unfortunately not only were mission institutions overrun, but missionary minds and methods as well. The process of creating Christianity in Africa was speeded up, but at the cost of releasing certain potentially deadly elements, such as irresponsible domination by one group and the turning of the church into a modern mass education machine. The compensation the foreign intervention gave to religion was that it opened the whole of Africa to Islam, which however adamantly refused to compromise herself. Before long we shall deal with the fate of Christianity and Islam under colonialism; for the moment we must go back a little and bring the story of Islam up to date.

CHAPTER FOUR

A Century of Muslim Theocrats and Holy Warriors

1. THE JIHAD IN WEST AFRICA

From the latter part of the eighteenth century till well on into the nineteenth, mighty movements for reform and expansion gripped Islam in Africa and often found expression in jihad or holy war. So far as West Africa was concerned, most of the leaders were connected with that mysterious group, the Fulani (who are also called Peuls and Fulbe), who had spread, with their cattle, into most parts of the savannah zone from the upper waters of the Senegal River to the marshes around Lake Chad. Some have remained pastoral nomads, and as one travels across West Africa one may see them at places thousands of miles apart with their flocks and herds, leaning on a stick looking proudly and without envy at modern man and his panoply of machinery. Others settled in the towns. Some remained "pagan"; others produced families of scholars of prodigious Islamic learning.

In the eighteenth century in the Senegalese Futa and Futa Jallon (in Guinea), Muslim reformers were gaining control in a number of places, setting up small centers of authority where God's rule could be fully exercised. The power in these theocracies was in the hands of people who could claim to know God's will. This was not through some special revelation but through their knowledge of the Qur'an, the traditions, and the law. In consultation with one another they could give a ruling in most situations.

In Hausaland, in such towns as Gobir, Katsina, Kano, and Zazzau, Islam had already had a long history. From the "Kano Chronicle," for instance, it is possible to get an idea of the process of Islamization. We hear that in the second part of the fourteenth century Muslims came to the town of Kano and advised the rulers to become Muslim. They taught people how to pray, appointed a muezzin to call the faithful to prayer and an imam to lead the prayers, appointed a man as butcher to make sure that animals were slaughtered in the correct Muslim fashion, and laid out a mosque area under a tree—possibly one of the old sacred trees of the pre-Islamic religion. A member of the rival ruling class defiled the mosque, and the two groups had to set up patrols, one against the other, the Muslims trying to keep the defilers out and the non-Muslims trying to make life difficult for those who wished to pray by committing nuisances and making a noise. Eventually, by means of prayer and a miracle, the Muslim group was in this case victorious, but even after this there were relapses. In the fifteenth century teachers from Mali and Bornu came to Kano, and the basic Muslim studies of jurisprudence and of the traditions of the Prophet were augmented now by the study of dogmatics, that is, of theology proper. Muslim customs as to the seclusion of women were very slow in being applied in Hausaland, and some people would say that even now they are not very well kept in many places. We also hear of the introduction of public ceremonial prayers at the time of the great Muslim festivals.

It is not easy to say how far or how deep Islam had gone before the reform movement which we are about to study. In modern times there is evidence of the survival of superstitions, of spirit-cults (the *bori*), of the uppishness of women, and other un-Islamic proclivities among some sections of the population, but the visitor to Hausaland can have little doubt that he is in the household of Islam.

The reformers, chiefly the great Shehu Usuman dan Fodio (this is the Hausa name—in Arabic he was called Sheikh Uthman Ibn Fudi), his brother Abdullahi, and his son, Muhammad Bello, have left writings in Arabic which cogently present their side of the case, though we must allow for their natural desire to paint a picture as dark and unhappy as possible of the state of affairs before they stepped onto the stage. The Shehu led a hegira (migration, withdrawal) out of the kingdom of Gobir in 1804 and in a series of engagements, after his declaration of a holy war, defeated a number of the Hausa monarchs. Typically enough, he himself retired to a life of prayer, study, and contemplation as soon as he could, and died in 1817, but his brother Abdullahi (d.1829) and his son Muhammad Bello (d.1837), with a dozen allied emirs, controlled an area of no less than 180,000 square miles.

In their apologetic the Shehu and his colleagues drew on the teaching of the Qur'an, the examples of the four rightly-guided caliphs, and the decisions of the great Maliki jurists. Especially they were able to cite Muhammad Ibn Abd-al-Karim al Maghili al Tilimsani, who had died three hundred years earlier. The gist of their argument was that there is an easily discernible difference between that which is *halal,* the permissible, and the *haram,* the forbidden. The task of a good ruler is to fear God and follow the rules of Islam, to command the right and forbid the wrong. He must have proper officers who will assist him—a wazir who will keep him from laziness, negligence, and blindness; a supreme judge who will enforce the laws for powerful and powerless; a police chief who will work with him; and a treasurer who will collect taxes according to Muslim law and look after the treasury properly.

On the other side, the rulers of the unbelievers (and people who call themselves Muslims but indulge in polytheism and refusal to ensure that Muslim law be recognized as such) are like beasts, ruled by their lusts. They succeed to the throne by mere heredity or force, are not chosen by the faithful as the best person for that work. They thrust themselves forward for office, they enrich themselves with un-Islamic exactions in the courts and the markets, they live luxuriously, they allow people to eat, drink, and wear what they like. They refuse women their rights, making as many as a hundred women subject to one chief woman. They tell their women to obey them, but fail to tell them their rights and their first duty, which is to obey God and his Prophet. Muslim law says an adulterer, if married, shall be stoned; if he is not married, flogged; that a thief's hand be cut off; that a deliberate murderer shall be killed but a homicide by accident pay blood money. These people harshly exceed those punishments. They force believers to serve in their armies and fine them if they refuse.

They do not help the needy. They prevent believers from wearing turbans and veiling their women. They pour dust on their heads, going to excess in self-humiliation. They beat all kinds of drums all night without purpose, whereas true Muslims only beat certain drums and then with intention.

In the face of such bad behavior a true Muslim is forced to emigrate and, after due deliberation, gather arms for a holy war. The reformers insisted they had not at first addressed themselves to the kings of Hausaland; on the contrary, the people had gathered round them and the kings attacked these bands of the faithful. Outnumbered and underarmed, Allah gave them the victory. Since the kingdom has been given to them, they must build the perfect Islamic state and bring the law into everyday effect at every level.

The Shehu and his colleagues and successors took over Zaria, Katsina, and Kano and extended their rule to Adamawa in what we would call the Cameroons. They were beaten off by the kingdom of Bornu-Kanem near Lake Chad. Their learning and the centers of their empire at Sokoto and Gwandu greatly impressed European visitors such as Heinrich Barth, who saw them about a generation later. Scholars of our own day have acclaimed the Shehu and his brother and son as brilliant philosophers of revolution and gifted ideologists who used social engineering as well as Islamic law to try to build the perfect Muslim utopia.

Much of this empire was still standing when the British came up, and they incorporated it with a minimum of change into their system of indirect rule. Some fiery modern Nigerian students will give a somewhat irreligious interpretation of the jihad and the empire that followed it. Those who have worked with and met Hausa Muslims have found many of them to be profoundly religious and deeply Muslim, humble, solid men of God.

We have seen that Shehu Usuman dan Fodio's reform was part of a much wider movement within Sudanic Islam: it was an inspiration to other leaders in the general movement. Also involved in that movement was Al Hajj Umar Ibn Said Tal, born around 1794 in the Senegalese Futa. He went on the pilgrimage to Mecca in his thirties and returned by way of Bornu and Sokoto, where he is said to have visited Muhammad Bello. On his return to the west he found increasing European encroachment coming up from the coast. It was not yet by way of military infiltration, but European goods were being brought in and sold in many upcountry places. Al Hajj Umar resisted this intrusion of things European, but saw that he would need arms to help him in the resistance. He therefore bought as much European armament as he could get hold of and used it in building up his own state. It would be wrong, however, to overemphasize this use of arms, since in his own view Al Hajj Umar was seeking to build up a truly Islamic state; and he himself emphasized much more the spreading of the true faith amongst bad Muslims and non-Muslims, and used warfare as a means to this end. At the time he was killed, in 1864 or 1865, his sphere of influence stretched from the Futa Jallon all the way to the Timbuktu area, and he had become in the eyes of his followers and of many people something of a superhuman figure. His memory is still held sacred among people there, some of whom even seem to hope that he will return to renew the great heroic days of the past.

We come next to the state built up by Sheikh Ahmadu Bari of Masina, that being the area along the Niger and its tributaries southwest of Lake Debo. Sheikh Ahmadu was in Hausaland in 1805, helping with the great jihad there. He returned to his own area but fell into severe trouble with the rulers of Jenne. He was also attacked by the Bambara rulers and declared a jihad in 1818 against bad Muslims and non-Muslims. He received much support from the Islamized people of Masina and was given the titles Commander of the Faithful and Imam. He founded a new capital, Hamdallahi, where he laid down the main lines of what he took to be the ideal Muslim state. There was a full Islamic organization, where the learned men and the clerics had the proper weight in affairs that their learning warranted. Islamic law was brought into fuller use and courts set up over the whole area. The ideas of Islamic taxation and giving were also carried out. Sheikh Ahmadu was a most sincere and profoundly committed Muslim, who tried in every way to carry out the way of life of Islam. He had a great deal of difficulty, however, for when he spread his sphere of influence right up to the Timbuktu area, he found that a large number of nominal Muslims came under his rule, and it was very difficult indeed to improve the quality of their religion. It is sad to recount that in 1862 this model state was conquered by Al Hajj Umar. Although it was to some extent revived during subsequent years, when the French took it in 1892 it had fallen a long way from the high Islamic ideals of Sheikh Ahmadu.

Coming south and westward from Masina, let us briefly study the work of Samori Turi, who in 1873 took the town of Kankan. He was a trader who took to soldiering when his beloved mother was enslaved. During the next years, until the French overtook him in the late nineties, he built up an empire based on his capital at Bissandugu in Guinea, stretching eastward all the way to the Black Volta River and the Ghanaian towns of Wa and Bole. One may even hear stories about him and his adventures as far eastward as Sandema in Ghana. Some of his descendants used to live in Kumasi and regale visitors with tales of his manly prowess. It is interesting to compare the different points of view that are taken with regard to this great hero. Of course greatness does not always include goodness. The French writers of the colonial period and the Africans who suffered in the tremendous warfare and conquests of Samori held the view that he was a cruel and selfish adventurer. Other scholars who have looked into the matter very carefully indeed interpret his career as that of a patriot trying to save his country from the encroachment of the colonialists and to build up a state which would be able to resist their coming. They say it is inevitable that in the process many people should suffer. It is not for us to decide between these points of view, but rather to try to discern something about the effects of the career of Samori on Islam. He himself took care wherever he went to try to break down the apparatus and organization of the old pre-Islamic religions. At the same time, his wars of conquest were bound to lead to a breakdown of the old society and of the religions that went with it. Therefore we find that, although some of the best Muslims would not say that he was a good Muslim, he made a contribution to the expansion of Islam, not necessarily by his own hand, but through the unnamed crowds of Muslims who were in a position to spread their faith as his conquests passed by and receded.

2. EAST AFRICAN ISLAM DEVELOPS AND GOES INLAND

Away on the other side of Africa, Islam had been on the coast for centuries but had not penetrated inland. Suddenly, in the middle 1840's, the faith began to go upcountry, and by the mid-eighties, when the Europeans divided up and annexed Africa, Islam was actively affecting the lives of the countries we would now call Malawi, Zambia, Congo, Tanzania, Kenya, Uganda, Rwanda, Burundi, and the Sudan. In fact, some frightened Christians imagined a group of Islamic polities was about to cover a good part of those lands and thought the "Christian" occupation had saved the day. Actually, that Islam is strong in some of those countries is at least in part due to colonial policy.

The study of Islam in East Africa is made the more exciting by the amount of hitherto unknown literature in Kiswahili and Luganda which is becoming available to fill out the picture. (In West Africa the bringing in of manuscripts in Hausa and Arabic to the university centers at Legon, Ibadan, Kano, and Zaria is a similar story. Even short visits indicate there is also endless treasure at Dakar and in Paris.) We can take three works in Kiswahili which have been in print for some time as our guide to the process of Islamic expansion at this period.

A little way from the northern border of Tanzania, and inland on the highland above the coastal plain, lies the area called Shambala and Bondi. Here the long dynasty of the Kilindi kings held power till the German days, and a certain Sheikh Abdallah bin Hamedi 'l Ajjemy, who was born in the 1840's, collected local traditions and wrote up their story. The founder of the dynasty was *mgego*—his first teeth grew in the wrong order—and should have been killed as an infant. As a young man he was accused of *uchawi* ("witchcraft") and had to flee. Luckily he knew hunting *uganga* ("medicine," "magic") and became a famous hunter of wild boar. He was so generous and gracious and so clever a *mganga,* he was asked to become king. He now kept his equipment in a hut, and the dynasty added reputed war-charms and the power to bring up fog to their spiritual arsenal. We hear of the circumcision camps of the young men, of royal interments with the burial alive of slaves. (This was a sacral kingship custom which Ibn Battuta noted was practiced both by the Blacks and in China.) Gradually Islam begins to appear in the story: a man is keeping the fast, another is praying. (Alas, some barbarian took advantage of the crouched position of the latter to shoot him in the back.) The Muslim injunction that all men are brothers stands not far from the description of a blood-brotherhood ceremony in which one partner calls on the ancestors. Sheikh Abdallah, our author, takes a healthy Muslim attitude of disbelief in an oracle which has obviously been hoodwinked. A visit to the area in the 1960's and extensive inquiries among people who know that country well suggest that Islam there has grown stricter and purer since those days.

Further south on the mainland coast opposite Zanzibar a most interesting type of Islam developed between the 1840's and the German conquest in the latter 1880's. This was an influential area and time in matters religious, since the people who took Islam far inland used it as a base. It is possible to obtain a most lively picture of it from the Kiswahili *Desturi za Wasuaheli* (the customs of the Swahili) collected by the German linguist Dr. C. Velten, in the 1890's, which he published at Goettingen in 1903. This "Mrima" area was in touch with Islam in Arabia, and the Persian Gulf as well as the Comoro Islands. Islamic law, belief, and practice of the purest quality was present there. At the same time the old African Traditional Religions were alive and active. The outcome is difficult to describe. Partly it is a parallelism with some convergence, where the two religions exist at different levels in people's lives. Thus the *mwalimu,* the teacher, is a Muslim official who teaches Qur'an, supervises the mosque, acts as registrar and notary of marriages, adviser on law, and medical consultant for some diseases. The *mganga,* wrongly but regularly translated as "witch-doctor," is a healer and "putter-together," with knowledge of herbal and spirit powers. He can treat a barren woman with whom the *mwalimu* has failed, giving her various medicines made from leaves collected in the forest or diagnosing which spirit is shutting up her womb. A young man conscious that his *membrum virile* is not as big as it should be can get the *mganga* by sympathetic magic to coordinate its growth with a fast-growing gourd. (Doctor and patient have to take the greatest care to arrest the process before it does too well.) Quite often the two religions supplement and reinforce each other. This is not syncretism, the pouring together of two things, but a using of both systems—as when one takes out two insurance policies.

By way of birth rites a child undergoes the Arab shaving of the head and offering of sacrifice with the Muslim reciting of various prayers in its ears, as well as a good African "outdooring," when it is shown to the elements of sun, moon, and rain, and the ancestors are remembered. A boy attends an African initiation camp and learns some robust songs and dances concerning sex and manners, while his circumcision in the bush fulfills the custom of Islam, and his reintegration into society may be marked by a *maulidi*—a celebration with Qur'an recitation. Clearly, however, purer Islam was gaining ground: where formerly *pombe,* beer, was served in a boy's coming-out ceremony, now festal food is put before guests. The Qur'an school is clearly much more important in a child's life than the initiation camps.

Certain practices stand in an ambivalent situation. The *pepo* cult is widespread—a person, usually a woman, feels afflicted and consults a practitioner, who tries various remedies and then diagnoses that she has a *pepo,* a spirit. The members of the cult gather and with much drumming and chanting bring the *pepo* to her head, talk to it, and then try to drive it out. Jesus' type of Christianity would have understood it well, but Victorian Christianity tended to refuse to discuss "such nonsense." In Muslim Africa similar cults, like the *bori* in Nigeria and the *zar* spreading from Ethiopia toward Egypt, have posed a problem. The *pepo* can easily be aligned with the *majinni*— the jinns of the Qur'an. However, increasingly the accepted Muslim attitude has been to tell people to trust in Allah and ignore the *pepo.*

It was followers of this kind of Islam—tolerant, long-suffering, but capable of reform in due course—who went upcountry. "Swahili" Islam has been likened to the rain from the Indian Ocean: it comes gently but persistently, and in the end goes deep. The Swahili was in the beginning a fisherman, he learnt patience and cooperation with the elements around him. (This was in contrast with Nubian Islam, which came into East Africa from the other direction and may be likened to fire. The Nubians were soldiers.) By the early 1840's the Swahili and the Zanzibar Arabs had regular caravans to the area of Tabora (in central Tanzania); by the end of the fifties they had organized Ujiji as a trading center on Lake Tanganyika, and stray groups had reached the Atlantic. By the time the European and American explorers came up in the 1860's they had deeply penetrated the western Congo, traded regularly with southeastern Uganda, and had met the forward group of Muslim traders and adventurers coming up the Nile from the Egyptian direction.

In the autobiography of Hamid bin Muhammad al Murjebi, nick-named Tippu Tip, perhaps because of his rapid gunfire or perhaps in honor of the Indian sultan who mauled the British, we can follow the story of one of the chief adventurers who traded from the coast up to Lake Tanganyika and beyond into the Congo from the latter 1860's on until the European take-over. He was of partly Arab and partly African descent and could be easily received by both societies. An educated and cultivated man, gracious and hospitable to missionaries such as Livingstone, ruthless with those who crossed his purposes, his main aim was trade. Ivory brought good returns; slaves were needed to carry it. Tippu Tip had at times to kill and capture, but he did it always with an end in view, and he brought some good with him. Some of the people who joined in on the fringes of Arab-Swahili enterprise seemed to lay waste countrysides by fire and sword with no great purpose. Tippu Tip found himself administering a large territory from Lake Tanganyika to far over into the Congo area, at first on his own behalf, but in the end as an agent of King Leopold.

It does not look as if adventurers and traders of this kind made any deliberate attempt to propagate Islam. They were new and dashing men, full of bravado and personal courage. They appeared with new ideas on trading and organization, with new weapons and tactics which they could use with deadly effect. They had new products and new techniques. To the East African hinterland they brought better breeds and methods of animal husbandry and rice growing; also the mango, the orange, the guava, the avocado, the tomato, cassava, and various beans and cucumbers. (Mangoes, oranges, and rice came originally from India. The Portuguese had already brought new kinds of maize, tobacco, various root crops like cassava, and the groundnut from the Americas to the coast. The boiling banana had come from East Asia.) The Arab and Swahili coming upcountry had dignity, poise, and self-assurance. The name of Allah was on their lips, and he seemed to permeate their life and thinking. Naturally people were curious about the element that ultimately made them the men they were. Gradually they would begin to explain about Islam, and people —especially manly young Africans—would join in and learn more and teach others.

3. ISLAM REACHES BUGANDA

The course of events in Buganda, a highly-organized African kingdom situated by the central western shores of the great lake which the explorers called "Victoria," we are able to trace in considerable detail thanks to copious material written by Baganda and the survival of an active oral tradition. Islam entered the area in the reign of Kabaka Suna, who died in 1856. Muslim traders and adventurers from the east coast came around the great lake and approached Buganda from the south. Apolo Kagwa, one of the leaders of the kingdom into the era of modernization and himself a Protestant Christian after beginning with the Muslims, tells how a Swahili trader rebuked the king for executing so many people, when all men are created by God and God had given him the kingdom to care for his people. In a Muslim oral version of this story he said, "All men are Allah's slaves"—that is, the king himself was liable to retribution for bad treatment of someone else's possessions.

Islam made rapid progress in the first years of Kabaka Mutesa's reign. He had come to the throne in 1856. He encouraged the use of Muslim greetings, keeping of the fast, the saying of the prayers, and the learning of the Qur'an. Men were now free to be circumcised if they wished—this had formerly been looked upon as disgraceful and is still not liked by the Ganda. The king did not submit to it, since in Buganda as well as in Ashanti, even in modern times, it runs against traditions of sacral kingship. The free running about of dogs kept for no definite purpose was discouraged. The Kabaka carried out a large-scale persecution of followers of the traditional spirits, who opposed the innovations.

Suddenly, in the 1870's the king turned against Islam. Perhaps Muslims of a sterner sort from the Egyptian direction had found fault with the alignment of his mosque, with his uncircumcision, with his leading of the prayers or his improperly butchered meat. It is also probable that Mutesa, who was one of the cleverest statesmen the century produced, was retreating from a policy which would inevitably weaken the Kabaka. Hundreds of young Muslim Baganda were put to death for their deviation from the old ways.

Mutesa called in Christian missionaries, who arrived in 1877 and

1879. From then until his death in 1884 he skillfully played off Catholic against Protestant, Christian against Muslim, and the new religions against the old. Under his son Mwanga, a less successful manipulator, the Christians went through the fires of persecution, and then Christians and Muslims joined to drive Mwanga out.

The next part of the story can be told by an old Muslim warrior, Usumani Wamala, who is now dead but who was interviewed and tape-recorded in 1967. The following is the substance of what the old man had to say.

I was circumcized after the death of Kabaka Mutesa, at a period when men were becoming Muslims in secrecy and one by one: they held meetings among the *matoke* [banana] trees. Natete, where the king had in the beginning located Muslim strangers when they arrived, was still a center for Islam. The people of Buganda of their own free will initiated the Arab religion, for the Arabs were merchants, not religious teachers. Many of our people on joining Islam also took to trading and teaching Islam at the same time.

The Kabaka made a plan to isolate the Christians and Muslims on an island in Lake Nnalubaale [Victoria]. We grew suspicious and refused to take canoe to the island. The Muslims moved up to Rubaga [the hill next to the palace] and attacked Mengo [the hill on which the Kabaka lived], while the Catholics attacked from the Kampala side [a hill on the other side]. We, the readers, [the people studying Qur'an and the Bible] were at last making ourselves public, the people of religion were toppling over the Kabaka. On ejecting Mwanga, we put in little Kiwewa.

The people of the three religions were cooperating. They held a meeting to share out the offices: the Katikiro [prime minister] was to be a Catholic, the Mukwenda [minster for the Singo area] a Protestant, and the Pokino [minister for the Masaka area], the Omujasi [minister for the army, a term from the Arabic], and the Kawuta [head of the royal kitchens] were to be Muslims. Later, some Catholics went back on the agreement, and the Muslims allied themselves with those without religion [that is, the followers of the old traditional ways] to make war against the Christians, who were driven out. The Kabaka [Kiwewa] summoned us, and our chief men attended. One of them was castrated and then shot. Others of our leaders were shot down. We heard the gunfire and supposed our leaders had been murdered, so we stormed the palace and chased out Kiwewa. Since we were now in charge, we were looking for a person to make into the Kabaka. Kiwewa had not been circumcised, things had been hurried, and at heart he was not a Muslim. When the sun came up, we made Kalema Kabaka and we drove out the Christians. We were in charge for over a year.

The Christians regrouped and fought us. We won some battles but were driven back. While we were retreating, Kiwewa, who had been captured, was killed, and some ten princes and fifty princesses who were prisoners were burned to death.

When we had been defeated, the Arabs who had helped us locked themselves up in their guesthouses in the same way that the foreign helpers of the Christians had done earlier, for instance, Mackay [a Scot serving with the Church Missionary Society] and Mapera [Père Lourdel, the French White Father]. Those Europeans had eventually been given freedom to escape to their friends by the Muslims. But the Christians killed the Arabs, they burned them at the guesthouses at Natete, although they had the status of guests. Afterwards [Lord] Lugard was angry that this had been done, but they were already dead.

Kalema retreated from place to place and then established his capital at Kijungute. There our Kabaka expired. We took Mbogo, son of Suna and brother of Mutesa, as our head. The Christians were still fighting us and drove us towards Bunyoro. Some while afterward Lugard sent ambassadors to tell us he wished Mbogo to eat Buganda (become Kabaka). Afterward he came to confer with Mbogo accompanied by Nubian soldiers. The white man sat near us—as we are sitting —and said: "Bwana Mbogo, do not allow death to come upon yourself and all the people who are with you. So much blood should not be spilt. I have come to bring you together."

Mbogo agreed, and Lugard inquired whether we all agreed. He inquired whether villages should be given us and we all agreed. This county [Butambala] was given us, and we laid down our arms.

The old man has telescoped the narrative somewhat and his general sweep in places contradicts the exact historical sequence of events, yet he gives an impression of the breathless high adventure of those days of revolution when he was young. In December 1890 the arrival of Lugard had announced the beginning of the colonial period. It had been a marvelous century for Islam throughout Africa, and though it ended gloomily, with the so-called Christian powers taking over, a mighty resurrection lay ahead.

CHAPTER FIVE

Colonial Fever to Freedom Regained

1. A SKETCH OF THE HISTORICAL BACKGROUND

To some of its victims, colonialism is on a par with the slave trade for iniquity. For its main exponents it was the expression of the highest ideals of a mission to civilize, involving the utmost sacrifice for little reward. To a social historian it is one way for a society to enter the modern world, comparable with the Industrial Revolution in the West or communism in Russia. There is some truth in these and many another generalization. Outsiders to Black Africa had hovered round her for centuries, and then suddenly in the nineteenth century began to thrust through into the hinterland.

A group of Albanian and Turkish adventurers took over Egypt, and under khedival authority there was a push up the river which brought the khedive's agents right into Uganda. The sultans of Muscat and Oman in Arabia had long had an interest in the East African coast. In 1840 the sultan moved his capital to Zanzibar, and within a few years his men were far inland, following up routes pioneered by Africans. The European powers had had African outposts but had not deeply penetrated the interior except in South Africa. Denmark was glad to sell her African forts, and Britain had considered withdrawing from the Gold Coast. There was a strong parliamentary lobby in

Britain, France, Germany, and Belgium against colonial commitments. Then, as if by a chain reaction, foreign countries pressed home their claims, and at a conference held at Berlin in 1885 lines were drawn on maps of Africa. The continent was divided up overnight, and then breathless Europeans spent the next years "effectively occupying" their territories. The United States had opted out early in the game. California students of *Chicano* background say this was because she was busy, like Russia, digesting internal colonies.

The Africans did not give in easily. Before the famous defeat of Europeans by the Japanese at Port Arthur in 1905, they had suffered Adowa (1896) at the hands of the Ethiopians and had learned a healthy respect for Ashanti and Zulu arms. Africa took years to pacify. Time was needed to build railways and roads and to set up riverboat services. Some of this work must rank amongst the engineering masterpieces of the age. As an example one may cite the Uganda railway from Mombasa to Lake Victoria, built by Indian labor with British money reluctantly subscribed. On the other hand, the suffering of the local Africans in places like the Congo eclipses the achievement of opening up the country. The rapids had to be circled by headporterage, then a railway built and revenue raised at the same time.

The colonial authorities strove hard to institute a cash economy, develop a labor force, collect taxes, and introduce the growing of raw materials which would sell and encourage outlets for their own manufactured goods. There was a revolution in public health. The secret was discovered of the malarial mosquito which had protected Africa from the white man for so long. Mass vaccination against smallpox was carried out, while the filtering and boiling or sterilization of water cut down on intestinal diseases. Flies were kept off meat, and the meat was inspected for worms. Cheap shoes foiled the jiggers but increased the number of misshapen feet. A monument to this side of the work of colonial authorities appears in the batteries of gleaming latrines which stand in prominent places in so many of the towns they built. A verse in Isaiah says, "Increase the people and multiply the joy." A variant reading inserts "not." The colonial powers and the Africans, to whom more children meant more happiness, certainly increased the people.

Things had begun to go more smoothly when another European civil war (1914–18) broke out. Africans were shipped off to France to fight in the trenches. The war was brought to Africa. The writer's father, who served with the Indian Expeditionary Force in East Africa, used to tell of the suffering of the "Kavirondo" porters sent from "British" East Africa into "German" East Africa. They were forced to march with loads all day and then given beans for their only meal of the day, a type of bean that needs to be soaked and boiled for many hours. The German commander ended up in Portuguese East Africa with more *askaris* (African soldiers) then when he started. These wars and goings-on can have meant little but suffering to the Africans. It was just that, from the beginning of time to our own day, it has been a human rule that people who happen to be stronger push other people around, and these in their turn, if they are strong enough, will coerce still others.

Things were recovering from the war when some foreign economic gymnastics called a slump or depression overtook Africa, and soon after that the Westerners had another of their civil wars. Africans again fought inside their continent and overseas, and again African development had to wait while resources were rushed to other people's conflicts. It was after World War II that the African freedom movement, spurred on by news of the independence of India in 1947, began to gather momentum. The year 1960 was a kind of *annus mirabilis* in which Nigeria, the French possessions, and the Belgian Congo followed such countries as Sudan and Ghana into independence. Much of the rest of Africa came soon after. It is no part of our purpose here to draw up a colonial reckoning. Already African scholars are beginning to do this from an academic and balanced viewpoint. It is now our task to try to pick out some of the main features of what happened to the three religions and what they did from the time of the scramble for Africa to the unscrambling of empire (1885–1960). After that we must deal briefly with the hectic decade since. Inevitably there will be some overlap and arbitrary pushing of topics from one section to another.

2. COLONIALISM AND THE AFRICAN TRADITIONAL RELIGIONS

To the best of the writer's slender knowledge, no one has taken in hand to draw up an overall, continent-wide account of what happened to the Traditional Religions during this time. This is no serious venture in that direction—only an effort to put forward and discuss some points about the fate of a few of them.

Friends and enemies have prematurely written their obituaries, but these religions are very much alive. Direct action can kill or severely inhibit vertebrate and highly articulated religions like Christianity or Islam in a given area over a period of time; but with religions like A.T.R. or Hinduism it takes subtler methods and long centuries.

The danger to A.T.R. was not really direct government action, though there was some of this. The journalists had made a lot of noise over "human sacrifice" at such royal cities as Benin, Kumasi, and Abomey, and in connection with shrines like that of Arochuku in eastern Nigeria. Military expeditions were sent to stop such activities and deal with various other issues. The mystery of human sacrifice had yet to be penetrated; in the West people still send their sons to wars, kill each other on the road, and enjoy accounts of bizarre, religiously tinged murders. The Victorians were sure of their own high culture, and while putting down "ritual murder" helped themselves to any available art treasures. These had, of course, been produced within the same system as the ugly features they were trying to destroy.

Government action was often based on ignorance. Thus a British governor asked the Ashanti for the Golden Stool (which enshrined the soul of their people) so that the great Queen might sit on it, and was amazed that his hearers went off glum and soon after took up arms.

Most unfortunately, the ignorance of colonial governors extended to African thought-concepts bound up with traditional religion. Thus time itself was seasonal and cyclical to the African; as his festivals came round he tried to preserve and repeat the good of the past. Colonial governments, on the other hand, thought in terms of a calendar year and an evolving sort of historical time which stretched on in a straight line as things got better and better through cautious innovations and careful, inexpensive planning. Again, African life was regulated by a law which had its ultimate sanctions in the spirit world, but all too often the colonial official did not seem to realize that customary law so much as existed, and imposed his own strange fiats from far away with the kind of remark one sometimes gives a child on a hot and dusty day: "Don't ask why. Do it!"

Not only in the early days but throughout the period, the Traditional Religions made some contribution to movements of opposition to the colonial governments. Here we see a more fearsome aspect of these religions, and we have to remember that when people are being terrorized and their soul ground down, their religions will not display mainly flowers and sweet odors. In 1857 the Xhosa killed their cattle and faced starvation, believing that through that sacrifice the spirits would come to their rescue and drive the white man into the sea. The men who in 1905 faced the latest German machine guns in East Africa with bows and arrows, spears, and a few outdated muskets shouted *"Maji, Maji!"* ("Water, water!"), indicating not only that they believed the German bullets would turn to water, as some informants will tell you, but as others add, also referring to a certain water which had bound them together. (We may compare the Allah-water and Yakan cult which was similarly used. Lugbara and Nubi informants say this water somehow bound the warriors to their heroic ancestors of old, who return to bring in a perfect age without the white man.)

In the matter of Mau Mau which contributed so much to Kenyan freedom, it will not be possible for some time for young African scholars to collect and analyze all the facts. A student of religion has to examine phenomena as they are, and though he has his value judgments, these must not prevent scientific examination. As a microbiologist at Makerere College remarked, one looks at a fine culture of *pasteurella pestis* and one's own likes or dislikes of bubonic plague do not come into it. In the case of Mau Mau, certain people who knew the traditional religion of the Gikuyu extremely well and were aware, either by instinct or study, of the findings of men like Pavlov, were able to set up a series of initiations and oath-takings including features which, by their very horror, brain-washed and welded men together. These men, almost without arms, were thus enabled to fight successful guerrilla campaigns against white men who brought up bomber aircraft and modern psychological warfare. Enemies of the movement, European and African, have emphasized the use of mummified penes and menstrual blood, etc., etc., but we saw in an earlier volume that these things have their context in religion and must be seen in that context. (The sexual parts of Kibuuka, the Ganda god of war, symbolized his strength; the *kunkuma* fetish in Ashanti made from menstrual blood, by its horror repelled bad spirits.) In any case besides elements taken from traditional religion and modern research, the creators of the movement were able to use a number of Christian elements as well.

In Buganda when the colonial governor deported the Kabaka, there was a tremendous revival of the old Ganda beliefs. Devotees gathered by the shores of the great Lake Nnalubaale, mother of the gods, and prayed, "O gods, who withdrew because of the atrocities of the white man, return at this time!" The ceremonies in the shrines of the Kabaka's ancestors took on a new lease of life.

As the modern independence struggle gathered strength, it could look to A.T.R. with a good deal of benevolence. If a politician were thinking in terms of projecting the African personality, it was natural that he should turn to traditional religion for help. But by definition the best and most thorough traditionalists could not, in many cases, do very much to bolster up modern politicians who owed their position to Western education and manipulation of Western ideological and political techniques. All too often people picked up odds and ends of African tradition. In Gold Coast/Ghana people "projected" by pouring libations at airports to welcome and send off friends. High-ranking visitors and politicians began to "outdoor" their babies.

Some of the politicians turned to the darker side of A.T.R., to some gruesome aspects strung together out of their context. It is said that some in Ghana consulted an oracle near Kankan in Guinea and paid reverence to strange images and objects. It is said that in another country further west, one politician tried to renew his strength and power by the ancient techniques of transferring these from a pregnant woman and a child about to be born. The deeper and more constructive meeting of A.T.R. with the African successors of colonial powers belongs in our next chapter.

In the matter of dealings between the colonial governments and A.T.R., history may have a vindication for the Europeans—as the people who cocooned A.T.R. Many British and French officials had a starry-eyed Rousseauesque attitude toward African culture as that of noble savages. If only they could be insulated from Christianity and education and coast politicians! Some modern Africans detest this as the "human zoo" approach, liking it as little as some autochthonous Americans like the word "reservation." It was not direct government action or inaction that most affected A.T.R., nor even the efforts of

Christianity or Islam, so much as the social, economic, and educational changes Western occupation brought about.

African Traditional Religions grow out of and interpenetrate the soil and community to which they belong and which belong to them. If the human ecology changes, a whole series of mutations takes place which affects the traditional religion. Thus if most of the youth are in Western-type schools, it becomes difficult to carry on the long-drawn-out forms of traditional education associated with initiation. Instead of a leisurely withdrawal, initiation into the being of the tribe, and reintegration as adults, there is a hasty circumcision during school holidays. If the young men are away at the mines, instead of proper courtship, ceremonial, and offerings to the spirits and to the component parts of the community, marriage becomes a hasty affair largely determined by how much cash a young man can produce, followed by long periods of separation. If real power is seen to dwell, not in the tribal heads and the elders but in some occasionally visiting, mostly absent official; if illness can be driven off by a few lizard-egg pills; then the spirits will not be as frequently consulted over the affairs of daily life. If clever cheap-Jacks talk continually of "science" and "progress," at a time when few people in Africa have much concept of the way other parts of the planet are being reduced to unspeakable ugliness and uninhabitability, the old quiet spiritual values of folk who have grown up close to nature will be held in disdain and young people will not learn them.

It is not easy for the healthy core of traditional religion to travel. When an African soldier who did not claim to be a Christian or Muslim died in Burma, all we could do was to salute the grave, fire off a few rounds, and sound the last post. Witchcraft, sorcery, and divination are available in the towns and slums, while the help and counsel of the traditional religious community in spirit and in flesh are not. Yet A.T.R. has vigorously survived. Its way forward into the future we shall explore later.

3. AFRICAN ISLAM UNDER THE COLONIAL HARROW

Many Muslims greeted the imposition of European colonialism with war: in Egypt the British had to bring up quite a lot of strength; in the Sudan they had some anxious times before they put down the

Mahdi; while in Somalia "the mad mullah" kept them busy from about 1899 till after 1920, when they ineffectually used aircraft against him. He died mysteriously soon after, perhaps of influenza. In northern Nigeria they had to overcome the emirs. In East Africa the young German colony had the greatest difficulty with the "revolt" of Abushiri Ibn Salim in the Pangani area in 1888, while in Uganda the Muslim Nubian troops rose in a "mutiny." The French seem hardly to have extinguished Muslim resistance in North Africa before it flared up again, while they ran into no small difficulties in West Africa. In the Congo in 1892, King Leopold's men had to fight the Muslims of the northeast.

In most Muslim areas there are those who consider that Islam, to be fully such, must have its own place where God's kingly rule can be fully exercised, a "Pakistan," a land of the Pure. Then there are some who feel that rebellion against or withdrawal from non-Muslim rulers are not live options, they are prepared to cooperate passively, if it is at all possible for Muslims to live their religion. Finally, there are some who will actively cooperate for the sake of the benefits to be gained, while looking forward to better times.

The French and British colonial officers of those days were fairly good at discovering how to win friends and influence people; and their study of Islam was much more advanced than their knowledge of A.T.R. They used force swiftly and effectively, and then guaranteed every protection to Islam. They recognized Islamic law in many places. In northern Nigeria, under indirect rule, they handed over to the control of the emirs large new areas and groups of people who had never been Muslim. There and in certain other places they did their best to seal out Christian missionaries, black or white.

In Buganda, as we saw, Lord Lugard (who was most influential in northern Nigeria as well) seems to have induced the Muslims to lay down their arms by promising to make their leader, Prince Nuhu Mbogo, Muslim Kabaka. They perhaps understood this to mean Kabaka of Uganda, while Lugard may have meant "Kabaka of a Muslim section of the country." In the end they were given a few counties and chieftainships. As he travels around Butambala County from mosque to tomb to Muslim home, a visitor knows he is in Dar-al-Islam, the household of faith.

Contrary to expectation, Islam spread rapidly during the colonial period; it was a kind of golden age of Muslim expansion. As old societies were broken up and the steamboat, the railway, and the model "T" Ford penetrated everywhere, Muslims from near and far traveled to formerly inaccessible places, carrying their faith with them.

A few of the bringers of Islam came from outside Africa. Thus teachers from Arabia had for centuries traveled by sea to Indonesia and then back to the East African coast. In Kampala in Uganda in colonial times and afterward, it was possible to enjoy the company of a sheikh who was born in Arabia, educated in the Dutch East Indies, and regularly traveled from Mombasa in Kenya through Uganda and Ruanda-Urundi to the Belgian Congo. He traded and taught as he went. He was a truly apostolic man, devoted to Islam, contemptuous of money and material possessions.

Muslims of British Indian origin gave considerable assistance in spreading Islam in Africa. The caravans of the century before had been financed by men from Kathiawar, Cutch, and Gujerat who had migrated to East Africa. Some of these were Muslims of the Shia group, of the Ithna-asheri type, and of the Ismaili persuasion, followers of the Aga Khan. Taria Topan went to Zanzibar as a stowaway in a sailing boat, became the sultan's chief customs officer, and was made a knight by Queen Victoria. His example, advice, and benefactions were of great service to African Sunni Muslims.

Seth Allidina Visram, another Ismaili, reached East Africa in 1863 and became a pioneer in opening up trade in Tanzania, Kenya, Uganda, and on into the Congo. His interests included the railways, lake shipping, stores, and the marketing of cotton, tea, and sugar. He died in 1916, having provided employment and encouragement for thousands of local African Muslims and given enormous sums to Muslim causes (his benefactions included Christians, too).

His Highness Aga Khan III, Sultan Muhammad Shah, himself came to East Africa in 1899 in time to hear of the defeat of the Kabaka Kalema and to see the swallowing of Muslim power by Britain and Germany. He came again in 1905 and called on Muslim leaders, including Prince Nuhu Mbogo of Uganda. His far-sighted plans for Islam were already beginning to take shape. He reorganized and strengthened his own people, who were now becoming indigenous in Africa, and commanded them to assist their African brothers. From their small *dukas* (stores) and growing businesses, help for African Islam went out—the employment of local Muslims, the encouragement to Africans to become Muslim, and financial help for the mosques.

The Aga Khan visited again in 1914 and 1926. In 1937 he called a conference of prominent Muslims in East Africa to discuss the future of Islam and set up in embryo the East African Muslim Welfare Society, which did not come into real effectiveness till it was reorganized in 1945. His Highness gave three million shillings (the shilling is worth about 15 American cents or 6 new pence British) and promised to match each shilling given by local people with an equal donation.

In the twenty-five years since then, this society has been a most potent agent for Islam, assisting in making mosques and Muslim schools of higher quality available over vast areas of Kenya, Uganda, and Tanzania. (The society and the Ismailis have also had contacts and interests in Congo, Mozambique, Rhodesia, Malawi, Zambia, and South Africa, but not on the same scale.)

The Ahmaddiyya also came from British India but were in about every other way different from the Ismailis. They came in the 1920's to Sierra Leone, Gold Cost/Ghana, and Nigeria, and to British East Africa. They have been the only Muslims who deliberately tried to give the Christians tit for tat. They honestly call themselves missionaries, and still do when some Christians have turned to jolly euphemisms like "fraternal worker." Robustly they match the barrage of insults which some old-fashioned Christians still put up, such as reflections on the Prophet's private life or the sexual pleasures of Paradise with remarks on the Virgin Birth and the mathematical nonsense of saying three are one. They make every use of modern Western education and organizational method.

The Ahmaddiyya are immensely good for Christianity in the way they purify her by showing her how she presents herself in some of her more gorgonlike postures. On the other hand, they have seriously alienated African Sunni Muslims in various parts of Africa by "sheep-stealing" and ruthlessly breaking up Muslim unity. In Pakistan, which is now their home base, the Sunni Muslims have been so infuriated as to beat up and kill some of them. African Muslims have been severely tempted to do the same. In long informal conversations in old-fashioned British Indian Hindustani with their missionaries at Saltpond in Ghana, Lagos in Nigeria, and Tabora in Tanzania it was possible to go behind the brash propagandist, Westernized front to meet the reality of these men. They are men of God who have made incredible personal sacrifices to fulfill their mission, as they see it, of bringing Islam to Africa. They believe that an African has a right to know his Islam directly, and they try to meet his needs in English if he can read English. They are also the chief translators of the Qur'an into African languages. The orthodox insist on Arabic; the Qur'an cannot be translated, they say. It is pathetic to an Ahmaddi to see a West African Muslim reading his Qur'an in an English paperback, edited by a Christian, or to see Swahili Muslims (till the Ahmaddiyya version came out) using a rendering by a Christian missionary. The Ahmaddiyya say that under pressure from their example the Sunni Muslims at last bestirred themselves to produce a Swahili Qur'an—at a time when Swahili Christians were rejoicing in a Jerusalem Bible at about a dollar a copy. They feel that one of their chief functions may be to stir the general body of Muslims into activity.

Apart from these few "fraternal workers" the people who have done most for Islam in tropical Africa have been very ordinary men and women who were not missionaries in the sense of being trained or sent by "home" communities, but rather in the sense that, as they traveled, traded, or looked after their homes, they lived out their lives as Muslims and encouraged others to join them. These humble folk have been of many different kinds. The class of person which the ordinary colonial subject in British or French Africa met as being in immediate authority was often a Muslim—the court interpreter, the policeman, the petty clerk, the ordinary soldier, the district commissioner's *major domo,* the storeman. Between 1957 and 1960 the writer interviewed most of the Muslim boys in Ghana who had reached the upper forms of the secondary schools. Most of them told a similar story. "My father was a Ga craftsman working at Elmina where he was converted by some Hausa policemen. As a government carpenter he traveled upcountry to Ashanti and married my mother, who also became a Muslim." "My father was a Fante clerk who was converted near Saltpond and for years served in Kibi, where I was born." "My father was a northerner who joined the army at Tamale. The sergeant major was a keen Muslim who noticed my father was a good soldier.

My father asked him how to become a Muslim."

Sheikh Shuaib, who was the leading Muslim teacher in Uganda, says that he went to Kisumu as a carrier for the British and was there befriended when nearly dying of dysentery by some Swahili Muslims who were in government service. He went to the mosque near the government headquarters at Entebbe and asked the Muslims to circumcize him. His first detailed knowledge of Islamic teaching was imparted to him by the Muslim cook of the local British officer. After initial training he was able to travel to learned sheikhs in other parts of East Africa and achieved no mean mastery of Islamic learning.

During the colonial period Islam was able to gain many adherents in the new towns which sprang up or grew out from older towns in many parts of Africa. A man coming in from the north to the "stranger quarter" of such cities as Accra and Kumasi found he had left his own religion behind, and that the people who befriended him were Muslims. He would carry home Islam to places in Togo and Upper Volta which had not known much about it before. As a visitor looks out from a high building at the fantastic expanse of Ibadan or Lagos in Nigeria, he sees some enormous mosques and scores of little places of Muslim prayer, for there too Islam has spread quickly among traders and immigrant workers. The same kind of story can be told for Nairobi, Mombasa, Dar-es-Salaam, Kampala, and many another city.

Under the colonial powers the Qur'an school was set up or continued to exist in many parts of Muslim Africa. In numberless cases it gave Muslims the only schooling they had. Sometimes a boy went on from Qur'an school to Western education. In either case it did much to shape a Muslim child's mind. A qualified person and his wife could set up to teach, she the girls and he the boys. If parents heard well of the teacher and he stood up to their cross-examination, they would bring their children. The pupils lived with the teacher, and though their parents gave customary presents, they worked his fields to earn their keep. The teacher knew the Qur'an material by heart and would write out pieces of it. Then children copied it onto their boards and memorized it by reciting it in singsong fashion. The instruction begins (in Arabic, of course) with the sacred invocation "In the name of God, the merciful, the compassionate" and goes on to the opening *sura:*

Praise to Allah, Lord of the worlds,
The merciful, the compassionate,
King of the Day of Judgment,
Thee we serve, thee we ask for help,
Guide us in the straight path,
The path of those whom thou hast favored,
Not the path of those upon whom
Comes wrath or those who err. Amen.

Then the pupils learn the five pillars of duty and their practice as well as the six pillars of faith and their meaning and a host of minute definitions and legalities. By example they learn the orderliness and cleanness of Muslim personal hygiene down to the last detail—with which foot first to step out of the toilet, when to shave pubic hair. In fact, they live an integrated Muslim life and can go on to further studies in regularly organized sequence till they themselves aspire to be teachers and jurisconsults, and to serve Allah in mosque and state.

The Qur'an school has come under bitter attack from some of those who know it best—modern young Muslims who have gone through it and on to Western schools. They say teaching methods were medieval—by threat, punishment, and rote learning. Much of it consisted of memorizing unexplained Arabic scripture and prayers. (The writer learned Latin the same way at a Christian mission school in India, so Islam has no monopoly.) The nub of their criticism is that Qur'an schools diverted Muslim energies from building up "useful" schools. It is said that the teachers put into parents' heads such nonsensical notions as that Western schools contradict Allah by writing from left to right or that, with the running water they provide, Islam will be washed out of their sons' heads. Yet not a few look back with nostalgia to their first "bush" Qur'an school.

There are other aspects of Islam under colonial rule which cause heated discussion among African students. Some say that the modified polygyny and comparatively easy divorce which Islam allows takes human nature rationally into account and is a sensible halfway house between the numerous wives a traditionalist could have and the one which is all Christianity permits. Good rights are guaranteed to women. For instance, Islam insists that women have legal rights and can inherit, whereas in many societies this is not so. Because of this Islam has been able to spread rapidly. This view is hotly denied by others who say that polygyny under a cash economy is only possible in the affluent circumstances of kings and princes and some Americans. (The polygyny of the last is presumably sequential rather than simultaneous, as an African colleague pointed out.) It is not a reality for ordinary people, though folk like to think so and try things.

Some young Muslims say with bitterness that the colonial period made African Islam conservative and obscurantist. Power in Islam was given into the hands of a lot of stick-in-the-mud old men. They buried their heads in the sand (or mud?) over modern education—especially science—in a way completely unlike the great days of Islam when the Muslims sought knowledge from Greeks, Christians, and others if need be, as far afield as China. The colonialists had been only too glad to let the Muslims sink into isolated and self-contented groups in the various countries, allowing them take over certain occupations such as butchering or lorry driving and have a species of autonomy. These young Muslims say the gerontocrats have really not tackled the problem of the relationship of Islam to African culture. They try to forbid most kinds of drumming and dancing and the drinking of beer, and have no concept of the value of African art. All they hang round their walls are cheap prints of the Ka^{c}aba.

The main contributor to these last remarks was a highly educated young Muslim who loved his religion most dearly and deeply. He spoke out of love and respect. Not long afterwards he was killed in a car accident. We shall see in the next chapter how some of these criticisms have already been met. It says much for the beauty and vitality of a religion when it can produce outspoken young critics as well as attracting new followers in their tens of thousands.

4. AFRICAN CHRISTIANITY UNDER THE COLONIAL YOKE

The attitude of the colonial powers to Christianity varied a good deal. The French government was at times anticlerical, and at all times there were sincere haters of Christianity to be found in all ranks of the French colonial service, yet most of the time the Christians could count on some help. Despite the agreements made in the 1880's and again in 1919 that African possessions would be open for religious work of all kinds, Protestants labored under some inhibitions because so few of them spoke French, and the French authorities liked people working in their territories to do so.

On the British side, most of the colonial officials were "public school boys" who believed in fair play and that religion was a jolly good thing, though one must not be fanatical about it. On the whole they allowed Muslims, Catholics, and Protestants freedom to do their work. On their side they considered that the Empire was good for missions, and on the whole, missions did the Empire good—though individual missionaries could be a confounded nuisance and Christian schools often produced "uppish natives."

The Belgian colonial authorities did not find it easy to forget that the Muslims had contested their hold on parts of the country and that Protestant missionaries had published reports in the world press of King Leopold's "atrocities" in the early years of opening up the Congo. Belgian Catholic missionaries (there were indeed few Belgian Protestants) were in any case naturally more acceptable, since they spoke French or Flemish. They accordingly received grants of land and subsidies for the work of education. The Protestants were able to call on very generous overseas help, especially American, to enable them to keep up.

The Portuguese authorities during this time gave missions a fair amount of freedom, though they tried to use Catholic missions fairly directly in their colonial policy of treating Angola and Mozambique as mere provinces of Portugal. Protestant work again suffered some disadvantages, which were compensated for by American and Canadian generosity.

On their side, contrary to the belief of some people in Africa today, the missionaries were not just running dogs of the hated imperialist. It is true that only a few raised their voices at the time against the colonial take-over, yet there were some righteous and prophetic men who did so. Many were conscious that it is against the basic tenets of Christianity for one group of men to lord it over others indefinitely, and they never failed to insist that colonialism was temporary, a way of preparing people to be their own masters. The thinking of these men, and direct African access to sources of Christian thought, meant that Christianity gave much service to the cause of freedom. It was, in fact, an essential ingredient of the bomb that blew up colonialism.

Most missionaries during the colonial period did not stop to think about the rights and wrongs of conquest, and they believed sincerely that they were serving the African. To opt out of every kind of cooperation with the government was impossible. In a way we stand on the other side of a chasm which separates us from previous human history. Till our own day it was taken for granted that the strong exercised power while the underdog suffered. We still allow ourselves cooperation with power structures we know are oppressing people we want to help. It is salutary to talk to old Africans about the hope and promise of a year like 1910 in, for instance, Togoland: "My German master beat me because I had not learnt my lesson. I dodged under his stick and gripped him round the middle. He started laughing and gave me the stick. Not long afterwards I was sent to Germany. Now when I preach there I always repeat (in German): 'It is work, work, that makes life sweet.' "

The colonial relationship was by no means all joy for the Christians. In the old precolonial days when they had worked by the permission of African chiefs, life contained fewer subtle temptations, but they had been free to carry on the work as they thought best or to withdraw altogether. Now there was negotiation between the government and their central organizations, then the field missionaries had to turn aside from gathering a congregation, building up a parish, studying the Bible with adults—and turn to education. The colonial governments had little money to spare for education, and especially in the Congo and in British Africa they knew that the churches could make that little go much further than a government agency. The churches had the know-how and the international and African contacts. They could call in highly qualified men from overseas to supervise the work; locally they could take responsibility, ensure continuity, rally loyalty and support, and muster gifts of free labor for clearing and building. On the Christian side, many welcomed this as a heaven-sent opportunity—Christian African parents especially wanted to have "their school." International commissions such as the Phelps-Stokes, which included Kwegir Aggrey of Achimota and had strong American support, recommended the link-up. Papal delegates and archbishops told their people to neglect all else for their schools.

Gradually the schools became more highly organized, and their range was extened from kindergarten to pre-university. Schools such as Achimota in Ghana and King's College, Budo, were set up as examples: but the Methodist Mfantsipim at Cape Coast or the Catholic Namilyango near Kampala were at least as good. The early missionaries had used the boarding school as a device for separating pupils from their "pagan" background. They had also carefully separated boys from girls, only partly because girls needed a different kind of education. Now the boarding-school system was extensively used because of the distances from pupils' homes and the lack of facilities for study there. (It is said that a White Father from upcountry came to visit and at night tried to blow out the electric light.) Going to a missionary boarding school does something to a man. It is rather like full infantry officer-training, or some years in a seminary. One learns to give leadership, yet work in a team; not to say the first thing that comes into one's head; to work endless hours and sit through tedious meetings in the garden of one's own thoughts. Nkrumah, Busia, Azikiwe, Obote, Nyerere, and Kaunda went to such schools. It was to the schools that the churches owed their tremendous increase of numbers between 1910 and 1960.

Yet there are many Christians who regret the investment of time, money, and men in schools. Roland Allen spent his last years in East Africa. He had been in Peking during the Boxer Rising when the foreign delegations were besieged, and he foresaw the end of colonialism and begged the churches to cease cooperating with governments, drop short-cut methods, and return to the way of the Apostles. Scholars of practical missiology who have closely studied such churches as the Church of Uganda find that in the early days the missionaries encouraged full and equal participation by Africans; in the work of evangelism they had to cooperate closely. The white man could pretend to little superiority when his very physical existence depended on the knowledge and generosity of his African colleagues. His contribution was useful, however, and plainly he could join in as a brother. Once schooling and European training became paramount, the European drew apart from the Africans; he was in those days manifestly better trained for Western organization and technicalities than they. By this time the European wife had come into it and naturally wanted to give her husband and children the kind of home and privacy to which she was used. Moreover, by contagion from his brothers and cousins in the colonial government, the missionary had in any case begun to draw apart. Leaving aside such theological and missiological considerations, a large number of African Christians ask us to compare some of the Christians of the older generation, many of whom were not well educated but were men and women in the best sense of those words, with some boarding-school Christians. They ask us to compare the school-managing ministers with the poor old catechists who bore the heat and burden of the day.

Another ancillary service which it is alleged almost engulfed too much of the Christian effort and produced too few results was Christian medical work. As soon as the White Fathers started in Black Africa they had it in mind to train Africans to be medical doctors. For instance, Joseph Atiman was born around 1870 in Songhai and captured as a child by slavers. He was freed by the White Fathers and in due time went to Malta for medical training. In 1888 he returned to western Tanzania and gave sixty years' service. Critics say it was of little more than the medical orderly type, but it was certainly devoted.

In Uganda Sir Albert Cook's pioneer work became the basis on which the great government hospital and university medical teaching unit at Mulago could be built. Fortunately the Church Missionary Society, behind Cook's work, saw in good time that it was better to have "Christians in institutions rather than Christian institutions" (apt slogans are their common coin), and encouraged government and academic resources to go ahead. At Lambarene, on the edge of the primeval forest, Dr. Albert Schweitzer was held up as a twentieth-century St. Luke, but by the end of his life an African medical man was heard to remark that the old gentleman was a paternalist and his hospital so lacked facilities as to be criminally behind the times. Nor had he trained African successors.

It is easy enough to overpraise or overcriticize Christian mission hospitals. The continuance of some medical service seems to be essential to Christianity. Jesus himself was a healer because he cared for the whole man. His followers can hardly do otherwise. Moreover, it is characteristic of much African thought to refuse to separate religion and healing. To this day some people prefer the comparatively poor religious hospital to the big, well-equipped public one. Many Africans like the text in Ecclesiasticus which suggests it is good to have a doctor who joins in prayer with the patient, for what he may not be able to do, God can.

Another noteworthy feature of Christianity in the colonial period was the proliferation of Christian churches, groups, and sects ranging from North American Pentecostalists to autochthonous and separatist churches. More will be said about some of the latter two later on; there has been such a plethora of writing about these churches in the last decade that it is difficult to add much to what has been so well and thoroughly done—some of it with the aid of computers and the latest methods of sociological analysis. It suffices to say something about one ingredient in this growth of churches which links up with the sacral kingship motif of A.T.R. Students in both Ghana and Uganda have been fascinated by the topic of leadership—what it is, and the cultus and charisma around it. Some of their findings on the religious connotations of *herrsherkultus* around a leader like Dr. Nkrumah are noted elsewhere. They found convincing evidence that Christianity in Africa in the colonial period had a leadership boom.

The African church leaders who stayed within the established churches and knew how to work with and command white colleagues were perhaps the most wonderful of all. Joseph Kiwanuka was born in 1899 and went through the seminary system to become a priest and a black White Father. In 1939 he became Bishop of Masaka as one of the first African bishops of the Catholic Church in modern times. In a colonial country with the white man in charge, he was in command of white men, yet such was the stature of his personality that to black and white alike he was father-in-God; he was, it is said, "color-blind." In 1961 he became archbishop. He spoke out boldly before the colonial governor, the Kabaka, and the postcolonial rulers of his country; he made fast friends with the Anglican archbishop and sought to end the enmity between the two major branches of the church in Uganda. It is said he refused a cardinal's hat. He rushed back from attending the Second Vatican Council in 1966 to die on his own beloved soil.

In the Ashanti forest it was possible in 1962 to call upon Prophet Samson Opong. He told us how, years ago, when he was languishing in prison at the hands of the colonial authority, he saw a vision. On his release he went about Ashanti preaching, and thousands responded. He visualized himself as a *gong-gong* man, the person who rushes round the village beating his *gong-gong*, calling out people to come together in service of the king. He asked the Methodist missionaries to work with him, and the names of their converts may be seen swelling the baptismal registers of the 1920's. Alcohol had been his weakness, and one day a malicious relative got him drunk and the prophetic power passed from him. He remained a humble church member to the end of his life.

Another outstanding leader was Reuben Spartas, who left his own church but founded the African Greek Orthodox Church in Uganda. He fought for an education, kept getting into trouble with authority, and particularly objected to the African being treated as a boy and not a man in his own home. He used sojourns in prison as an opportunity to study and teach. He was a self-taught church historian and finally sought communion with the Greek Orthodox Church, having helped to organize a church system complete with schools and a cathedral.

Leadership by women was not lacking. One secession of about 90,000 people from the Catholic Church in the area behind Kisumu in Kenya, where other churches had suffered much worse from hive-offs, was led by a most intense young lady, Gaudencia Aoko, who has the title of *mama mtakatifu* (Holy Mother) in her Legio Maria Church. (Experts in translation point out that it is the Catholic custom in Swahili-speaking East Africa to call the Pope *baba mtakatifu,* "Holy Father," perhaps because *papa* means "shark," *popo* means "bat," and *pepo* means "evil spirit.") She ranks high in a hierarchy with a Holy Father, cardinals, and archbishops. She receives visitors graciously, and although she does not look as if she had reached thirty, has power of personality enough to make a strong man quail.

Looking at leaders like this, who are presumably Christians till declared otherwise after due process, a visitor who has prayed with them in their different churches can believe that the gates of hell cannot prevail against God's church.

There is just time to mention a well-worn theme which occupied much Christian attention in the colonial period—Christianity and African culture. Much of the early work of evangelization was done by Africans, and they must have had some reason for making a clean break with a number of aspects of the old African culture. Christianity has some things to condemn in every culture—only its protagonists must make sure it is Christianity that is doing the condemning, and not their own cultural blinkers causing them to fall into a ditch.

In our seminar discussions the matter of polygyny kept coming up.

Its upholders can say that it is natural to man and that God accepted it in the patriarchs of the Old Testament. Nowhere is one wife enjoined in the Bible, except for bishops. (One literalist asked how some bishops dared *not* to marry, when the Bible clearly says, "A bishop *must* be the husband of one wife.") Modern Western governments allow divorce so easily that one man can, in a lifetime, cohabit with plenty of women. They asked whether it was the cultural blindness of Victorian missionaries, brought on them by the remnants of Greco-Roman customs which they wanted to give to Africans. It is not easy to recapture the words describing the beauty of the monogamous man-woman relationship in Christian marriage as expressed in an address to women given by the wife of an African archbishop. She went back to the Genesis story—God did not want man to be alone, so he made woman—not from his head to be his master, nor from his feet to be his slave, but from his side to be his partner and complement: that together, as two halves hinged into one, they might serve God, the man doing what she could not, the woman doing what he could not, and both working as one. Theirs was a lifelong exclusive partnership in which they expressed their love for one another and God through creating children and bringing them up to serve God and man. For young people entering marriage she prayed that they might love God, love and cherish one another, and go in due time through death's deep shadow without fear.

Marriage, has been mentioned, and it is necessary to say something of other "rites of passage." The church has been deeply concerned with customs surrounding birth and trying to keep infant baptism more meaningful than it is in the West. Africa may have something to teach the world about properly honoring and marking off puberty and the attainment of manhood and womanhood. In the colonial period African customs in these matters caused the church some difficulty. The so-called "female circumcision" in the milder form of clitoridectomy was usually overlooked in the hope that general education would bring its discontinuance. Where there was fairly widespread scarring or other possible threats to natural childbirth, or where the psychological shock to budding womanhood was feared, some missionaries resorted to bold interference with custom. This was naturally resented, and (for instance in Kenya among the Gikuyu) the retention of female circumcision became involved with a general movement of resentment against the white man. In some other places such as Zambia the educational side of African women's rites was built upon by giving girls Christian instruction on being a woman, wife, and mother.

On the male side there was a most interesting experiment in the Episcopalian Diocese of Masasi in southeast Tanzania. Here the Yao and Makonde and other tribes used to hold a circumcision camp for boys, during which a lot of valuable instruction on sex and manners was given, besides connecting the boys with the spirits of the ancestors through various ceremonies. In the 1920's Bishop Vincent Lucas of the Universities' Mission to Central Africa (a "High" Anglican group formed in response to David Livingstone's appeal), in consultation with his African clergy and some of his chieftainly cronies, devised a form of the rites which maintained the circumcision of the young men without anaesthetic but eliminated the ancestors. Instead Christian prayers and rites were inserted. It was claimed that the substance of the old instruction was retained and Christian teaching added. Some Africans have high praise for the idea. Bishop Masaba, who underwent the Gisu rites on Mount Elgon as a boy and has sought to Christianize the rites of his own people, considered Bishop Lucas' efforts a fine attempt. The Roman Catholics in neighboring areas have also used Lucas' ideas. On the other hand, a young Tanzanian priest remarked: "Unfortunately it fixes us in a moment of tribalism. We are a nation now, and circumcision is better done at birth in hospital."

It is natural that Christianity should have difficulty over death ceremonies in Africa, in that the modern West is so inadequate in the face of death. First of all, in most parts of Africa suppression of real grief and artificial expressions of mourning have not been encouraged. Secondly, traditional religion usually taught people that death was not the end but the gateway to another stage and form of life. Not many people in the West really believe that death is not the end, whatever they may say while the priest is around. The church in Africa all too often concentrated on substituting Christian rites and eliminating objectionable features left over from the past. For instance, in Ganda there was difficulty with *okwabya olumbe,* the series of rites by which death is torn up and abolished, and also with heir-naming ceremonies. The spirit of the deceased has to be set up in the spirit world, and plainly told that his possessions, his farm, his wife and goods, have begun a new life. This includes a ritual and symbolic act of incestuous sexual intercourse—a close relative jumps over the outstretched legs of the surviving partner. In some cases there is an exchange of male and female garments. The Native Anglican Church investigated the rites over a period of years and in 1919 nearly made a decision. It felt it could not abolish them, since people believed the widow and children might be made ill by the spirit of the dead man, and the whole corpus of ceremonies involved important considerations of heirship under Ganda law. Various alternatives have been tried. Thus it has been suggested that instead of the customary rites the body should be brought to church at once and a service and burial held. On a convenient day the heir should be proclaimed in church and prayers said for him. Then there should be a meeting at the house with the chief and the priest present, to complete inheritance formalities, and people should go home before dark. The widow is to be ceremoniously handed a Bible, and refreshment is to be tea and not alcohol.

Modernizing traditionalists among the Ganda take it that holding a wake with excessive beer drinking is an accretion to the funeral rites, and that the separation of the dead from the living can be effectively carried out either by other means or by a very strictly symbolical act. Thanks to the wisdom of Bishop Tucker, who tried to ensure that Africans should make their own decisions, and the knowledge of custom possessed by church leaders such as Apolo Kagwa, who was an adept at manipulating the facts of traditional lore, it was possible for the church in Uganda to deal peacefully with this and other problems. (The Ugandan Anglicans also substituted a tea party for a ritual battle in the enthronement ceremonies of the Kabaka—which shows how an Oriental drink may be sacramental for Episcopalians everywhere.)

Students studying the history of Christianity at Makerere University College in Uganda were asked to make a field study of the Catholic Diocese of Masaka, which is some seventy miles from the capital. Some worked on the history; others visited the churches, took measurements, and made notes on religious geography; others interviewed clergy and public leaders who had come from there; still others tried to investigate Christian marriage and the family in the diocese; while yet others tracked down art, music, and drama. The mission was founded in 1879, and the Parish of Villa Maria on the site of an ancient shrine in 1892. There and in the neighboring parish of Bikira (the Virgin), the White Fathers and White Sisters have worked. Bishop Streicher, an Alsatian whom the British feared, loved the place. There African orders have grown up for both men (the *Bannakaroli*, "brothers of St. Charles Lwanga") and women (*Bannabikira*, "daughters of the Virgin"—"daughters of the Ethiopian Eunuch" is said to have been considered as a title but rejected in the end). A hospital has been built. From near and far, Catholic families gather to say the rosary and attend Mass.

Young boys entered the nearby minor seminary and went on from the major seminary next door to study at Rome and further afield. Bishop Joseph Kiwanuka, who was mentioned above, presided from 1939 till 1961, when he left with regret to become archbishop. He encouraged experiment and full community participation in his schools. He encouraged Christian African art. Instead of vulgar Italian "church-shop" sculpture, he liked to see vigorous African wood carvings. Over murals and paintings things were held up a while as Africans hotly debated whether Jesus and the angels should appear with white faces. At first there was a period of compromise when they appeared with brown faces—suitable enough for inhabitants of first-century Palestine but easily confused by children with the features of the local Indian shopkeepers. Now black angels and Christs are as commonplace in art as they are in passion plays and pageants.

A school of actors and dramatists using Christian themes has grown up near Masaka. It is a pity that on the night of the grand climax of the passion play, we found that the Christ had gone to the airport to talk to a passing American foundation man about a scholarship, but the play is to be published in full. In the matter of music Masaka diocese is associated with the movement which has produced a full *martyrlogium* of music to be sung and played by a full Ganda choir and orchestra in honor of the Uganda martyrs. A Muslim graduate reported that when the Pope visited (in 1969), "Among the Catholics it was all drums and Ganda music, the organ was hardly heard." Oh, that there could be a symbolic burning of church organs to balance the old symbolic burnings of things African!

The present bishop and clergy of Masaka modestly say that they and their laity have still much to do in the matter of relating Christianity and African culture. It was years ago, still in the colonial period, that a Ghanaian colleague whose family service of the church goes back to before colonial times remarked: "No one can Africanize for us. First the church must make many thorough Africans who are Christians into thorough African Christians. They and the Holy Spirit will do the rest." It was a promise.

CHAPTER SIX

The Three Religions
and the Way Ahead

African Traditional Religions in many places survived the colonial episode as entities. A civilization as old as the African can swallow hard and allow a mere three-quarters of a century of superficial foreign domination to be assimilated into the system as an interlude. In the ten to fifteen years of independence, African hands have dealt some deft blows at a number of A.T.R. systems. Many of them found their key point in sacral kingships. There are fewer sacral kings around today than in colonial times. They have been abolished in Rwanda, Uganda, Tanzania, and other places, and their position modified in Ghana and Nigeria. Modern African politicians will be much less tender with beautiful remnants from the past than colonial officials were. African Traditional Religions can hardly live on for centuries in a few odds and ends left over from complete chains of symbols, such as boys' puberty circumcisions or the activities of "medicine men" and "witch-doctors."

It is possible that the A.T.R.'s will survive by organizing a neopaganism of the kind that arose in the Greco-Roman world in the third and fourth centuries, associated with the Emperor Julian or with the Roman aristocracy. In some parts of Africa such revived and reformed groups are emerging. Often they claim to be monotheistic, are high in ethical and philanthropic values, and have an organization not dissimilar to that of the church. So far they have not produced a leader who can organize them on a nation-wide basis, but if they threw up a messiah and events assisted him, a continent-wide movement might emerge.

Can the traditional religions use Islam as their vehicle into the future? In the past both European scholars and African Muslim reformers have mocked African Islam for being a mixture with A.T.R. From interviews with sheikhs in places such as Dakar, Accra, Kano, Omdurman, Nairobi, Tanga, and Arua, an investigator is bound to doubt whether ultimately Islam will compromise. The whole rhythm of her history is that "there cometh a time of reformation." Sooner or later a cleanser and purifier arises, and non-Muslim accretions are ruthlessly thrust out. On the other hand there is a good deal in Islam which is echoed and paralleled in a number of the traditional religions. For instance, circumcision or the existence of hierarchies of spirits, some of which are like angels, others like *jinn*. Many African customs can sail into the future under the lee of "Islamic" customs which are really remnants from the pre-Islamic days of the Arabs.

Then there is a category in nonfanatical Islam which permits the existence of things not asked about. "Your Lord has laid down a few things which must be. He has forbidden some that must not be. Rejoice in his mercy and do not ask about the rest." This permits two systems to coexist in a symbiosis over some areas of life, like a sea anemone on a crab or tickbirds with a herd of cattle.

African Traditional Religion will above all make itself felt in the ideologies produced by Africans, such as that of the Ghana philosophers, whose work was impinged upon by the Nkrumahists but continues after their expulsion. The African is a person closely attuned to nature, who lives in harmony with the sky, the plants, the animals and spirits around him. The earth is a mother who, though she is loving, is also awesome; she is not to be raped but treated with affection and deep respect. The African lives in close and intimate participation with his family and neighbors—in a way he is not an individual but part of a group unconscious. He partakes of a common life which he shares with those to whom he is related by ties of blood or culture. Till recently outsiders said he had no history, but in reality no one is more acutely aware of the long stretches of the past and the ever-presence of those who have gone before—the time-loadedness of the present. He is aware, too, of those who are to come after him. He must not contradict the past nor speak and act in such a way that those to come will have to gainsay him.

According to this system of thought *homo africanus* dwells in a universe of power in which he has his due place. Others, by wrongly manipulating power, have broken into his harmony, but inevitably they have been ejected. He cannot forget but he bears no hate. The African's task remains to bring totality of being and the secrets of the balance of the powers to other men everywhere.

Similar ideas have been taken up in the Bantu-speaking world, by a number of young thinkers who also know the writings of Leopold Senghor and the *négritude* group, though they could not go forward with certain parts of them. There is a further interplay of thinking with Julius Nyerere and Kenneth Kaunda. African man is a corporate being interrelated in wholeness of life with his family, his local and national group. For hundreds of years mankind has progressed by one-sided pushes, by thinking problems through after removing them from their context, by ruthlessly thrusting through to solutions. Now the African insists on seeing things whole, on experiencing a situation with his whole being, on carrying the group with him and working through every member in oneness. Africa is one, so also is mankind. Each individual human being finds his fullness by fulfilling his due part through his life and work and his sensitivity to his proper place in nature and the world. The earth and one's fellow humans must not be exploited or ignored; their agony or poverty is eventually passed on to all. The depredations of the violent and the exploiters have to be opposed and stopped.

Thus when the question is asked, "Will A.T.R. survive into the third millennium?" it is reasonable to reply, straight-faced: "How can you destroy it? Shall we shoot every African?" For A.T.R. is not a close rational and logical chain of belief and practice like Islam, nor an arch with a keystone like Christianity, nor a social banyan tree like Hinduism. It is features of African minds and lives. It is most hospitable. Once when the Lord Mukasa, he, the great one of the Lake who had obviously been the head of the Ganda pantheon at one time, was speaking through a medium, someone asked him: "What of the Christians and Muslims?" He replied, "They follow Katonda. There is no rivalry between us."

Islam will be able to survive in Africa apart from A.T.R. in the end, but Christianity of her very nature must be grafted onto native stock or she will remain forever foreign. Then her best hope will be that Africans become integrated into the mass of modern secularized humanity which has no indigenous culture of its own. Christianity has a great deal of experience in secularity. Before that terrible fate overtakes her, Christianity must positively recognize her role as a vehicle for A.T.R. It is not only in the thinking of leading Christians such as Busia, Nyerere, and Kaunda that she will help to preserve and cross-fertilize with traditional values. Christianity will serve A.T.R. in other ways as well.

There are a large number of churches in Africa started by people who have seceded from the churches brought from the West. It has been said of these churches in disdain that they are bridges by which the African found his way back to paganism, or that they had to be studied because to preserve the health of the body one has to study pathology. Many of them were basically an attempt to break the European mold and express Christianity in an African way. They are often in essence and intention Christian. In the end it has been difficult to deny the title to the Musama Disco Christo Church in Ghana, which has a sacred locality where with great gusto festivals are celebrated such as Christmas and Easter, plus some never heard of before, such as "the Peaceful Year" and "Akaboa's (founder's) Birthday." A service may last for hours and include singing, clapping, dancing, speaking in tongues, preaching by a charismatic leader, Bible reading, and healing. Prayers can be set or extempore, monologue or antiphonal, and include wrestling with spirits. Similarly it is hard to reject the title of Christian for the Church of the Lord, Aladura, which flourishes in various parts of West Africa and was found after years of careful investigation by a New Zealand theologian to exhibit in full measure the classical marks of the church.

In 1968 the relevant committee of the World Council of Churches meeting at Canterbury agreed to admit the Kimbaguist Church. The road that church had followed seemed a long and terrible one. In 1921 Simon Kimbagu appeared in the Congo saying he had seen visions and had authority to bring men to God. He gathered twelve disciples and went about healing the sick and preaching. The Belgian police came for him, but his followers hid him. Then he handed himself over. He was condemned to death, but they dared not kill him for fear of a tumult of the people. He died in prison thirty-one years later. His followers were said to have made him into a black Christ, to have introduced belief in various spirits, and to have brought in African ceremonials and rituals. They had refused to pay their taxes and committed other such crimes. When they were at last recognized by the Congo government and by the world there were said to be three million Christians of this type.

The best of the African religious ways of thought will increasingly be felt in Christianity as more and more young Africans study the Bible in Hebrew and Greek and the doctrines of the early church in Latin and Greek (some indeed can manage Syriac as well). The Bible seems to speak to them so directly, its thought-world is something they can grasp in a trice if there is not the distorting mirror which European exegesis sometimes provides. So many matters which Western scholars labor to explain because their senses have been dulled by living under artificial conditions, many an African understands almost instinctively.

In that continent there is a renaissance going on—a young African theologian at the university can be a manly man admired by "the girls," a poet, a musician, a generous eater and drinker (without being a glutton or a drunkard), and brilliant at his subject. He is one among a large number of others who will go out and run the government and the life of the country. Men like these are, in a way, an epitome of Christianity at its best, and they have been turning their thoughts to the problems of Christianity in Africa. They know that basically Christianity required only a few things as essential, and that it is a religion not of law but of spirit. The Apostles would have liked everybody to become a Jew before he became a Christian, but they soon abandoned that and Christianity went wholeheartedly into the Greco-Roman world—taking its language, its customs, social structue, and so on. In Mesopotamia, in India and China, Christ became "enfleshed"—"enhumaned"—in other cultures.

There is no such thing as a Christian culture, and there is no culture in the world which cannot be Christianized. It is true that when the church went into northern Europe she apparently imposed Roman and Latin culture. As some Ugandan Christians remarked with mock solemnity, perhaps the Franks, Anglo-Saxons, and Germans had no culture of their own—perhaps Nazism and European colonialist master-race arrogance is the price the world has had to pay for the church taking short cuts in Europe between the fourth and the fourteenth century. But Africanness cannot be thrust aside like that.

These young African theologians love Africa deeply; they are steeped in her ways, they talk and write her languages (not all politicians can), they sing her songs, dance her dances, and sound her drums. Men like these want Christianity really to take the plunge in Africa, no matter what the risks. They feel that if only old and conservative African leaders would stand out of the way, if only overseas friends would stop exerting any kind of control, Christianity would have a chance really to woo and win the heart of Africa—or to put it in their apt way: to produce "an organic and home-grown Christianity."

They point out that in many parts of Africa the Christians have accepted for the name of God the name of the local African deity who seemed to stand above the others—the so-called "High God." Other gods, high spirits, and spirit-manifestations, good and bad, were ignored. This was at a time when there was a certain tendency among Western theologians to overemphasize God as a transcendental person and to play down his more "faceless" presence immanent in his creation and its continuance. They fell into Satan's trap by loudly asserting that the devil did not exist.

Theologians in Africa are beginning to explain that they see God as spirit manifested at different levels and in different ways. Theirs is a world of thought where the great hierarchies of spirits and angels and principalities and powers of the Bible come to life again—not as a hard, literalistic ballet of bloodless metaphors, but as sheer poetry which takes the scales from the eyes suddenly to see the world dancing with the life of the Spirit in a new kind of reality.

The system is powerful in its divinity, for one begins to realize dimly that God is not just love but has certain strongly terrifying aspects. It is also a humanism, for the dualism of certain forms of Christianity is done away, and one realizes that man in some ways is sometimes more righteous than God at the limited number of levels at which man operates. That is one of the consequences of God making man in his own image.

These theologians are seeking to understand what African Traditional Religions, through exorcisms and the treatment of psychosomatic disease, are trying to tell Christians. They are also exploring forms of liturgy—and the art, music, and architecture that go with them expressing man's search after, and discovery of, the mysteries of God. The idea of the fellowship in holiness, the communion of people trying to live reciprocally the life of God's kingly rule, is also strong in this kind of thinking. These theologians grasp well the concept of a church community, harmonious and highly integrated, seeking to serve as a salting or leavening of the larger communities in which it lives.

Where foreign control did not quench the spirit, African Christians have been great missionaries. For instance, Baganda Christians sent men and women to teach Christianity to the tribes and districts around them; their Apolo Kivebulaya was an apostolic man who went over the mountains to preach to the Pygmies. The isolation of the mainland Chinese after the tragic dispersion of Nehru's dreams grows daily more terrifying for the future of mankind, yet in the Middle Ages much Chinese porcelain came to East Africa, and a giraffe traveled by junk to China. It will perhaps be men from Africa who save the day for mankind as a whole.

From the wondrous possibilities of what the African Christian theologian and evangelist will do for the world in general we must turn to more mundane things. At the time of *uhuru* the churches possessed the best propaganda machinery in nongovernment hands on the continent, and they were not slow in pointing out how much they had contributed to the emergence of the new Africa. This most Africans were prepared to admit in generous terms, but there were many who wished that the churches would purge themselves of their foreignness, cease interfering in things that did not concern them, and join in nation-building.

By "foreignness" they mainly meant the presence of foreigners in posts of ecclesiastical leadership. African churchmen were not going to be hurried to turn their friends out with indecent haste. In some cases their patience and courtesy has been almost suicidal. However, in most countries leadership is now in African hands, and in many places has been for a long time. Property has been handed over to the local ecclesiastical authorities. Considerable care has been taken to ensure that foreign financial help comes at the request of the local church and is given to the local leaders to use "without strings." The amount of money that has come in this way has been phenomenal, and Western Christians have set a better standard of giving than Western nations. Accepting foreign money may be dangerous, but one church has helped another with men and money, and the other has received with dignity, since the church began. The exchange of men and women workers and other forms of help is essential to Christianity, but it should work both ways. Perhaps nothing would do the churches in the West more good than a larger number of African missionaries.

Another element in the matter of "foreignness" is that the misdeeds of the "whites" in South Africa or Rhodesia and of the Portuguese in Guinea, Mozambique, and Angola seem inevitably to bring shame on Christians in other parts of the continent, even though the churches have denounced the ruling groups in those African countries and have done quite a lot to undermine tyranny in Portuguese Africa, even to the extent of supporting guerrilla movements. Perhaps African Christians can get their coreligionists in other countries to take a more active part in using the methods open to Christians to bring an end to situations such as these.

Critics of the churches want them to cease interfering in things that do not concern them. By this they largely mean politics. This is a thorny question. Jesus was asked a catch question as to whether people should pay tribute to Caesar or no. If he said "Yes," they would count him as a running dog of the imperialists. If he said "No," they would tell the Romans he was a rebel. He asked his questioners if *they* had a penny (presumably he did not carry such things) and inquired whose *image* it bore: it was Caesar's. (As a good Jew talking to Jews he could thus allude to the Genesis story where man was made in God's *image.*) He then replied, "Render to Caesar the things that are Caesar's, and to God the things that are God's." The whole man belongs to God. A Christian cannot keep out of politics, though every political cheap-Jack will misquote Jesus to imply that Christians should keep purely to spiritual things. Africans do not normally, except under Western influence, make this false dichotomy between spiritual and material things, for to them the two interpenetrate.

In Ghana in Dr. Kwame Nkrumah's day a highly-trained Christian minister who knew the attitude of Bonhoeffer and Tillich and other Western theologians to the church-and-state relationship joined the ruling party and became a member of Parliament. It was a time when Dr. Nkrumah was being given such titles as *Osagyefo,* which is a royal byname signifying his victory-bringing powers and in some connotations his position as deliverer. He was called "messiah" and choruses sung of Jesus were sung of him. A creed had been written in which his sufferings were paralleled with those of Jesus. The latter's words were reshaped by Dr. Nkrumah in such statements as:"Seek ye first the political kingdom and all other things shall be added unto you." Some Christians, including this minister of religion, refused to take alarm. They knew that in a land where many people were brought up on the Bible, one said: "Holy, holy, holy is his name," where others ignorant of the Bible might say: "He's a jolly good fellow." Also they could not see why Christian influence should opt out of helping to run the country in its hour of revolution, when it was heaven to be alive and young.

Other Christians protested and were told to keep out of politics. When the *coup* came, our man was put in prison and told to keep out of politics. Christians cannot keep out of politics—let us only hope they will continue to be found in every party. The Western working fiction of the separation of church and state may not be sufficient for the subtlety and honesty of African thought.

The other main sphere from which some people wish the churches would withdraw is education. In the countries where the churches have played a major role in education, the governments have taken steps to take over. Perhaps no other people in the world place so much emphasis on education as do the Africans, and ministers of education ask whether it is right that something so important should not be under the exclusive control of the elected representatives of the people. The churches in some cases have been reluctant to hand over, for this too is not an easy question. Often they have found means of compromise or of continuing to serve in some aspect of the work. There are vital sides of education where Christianity's world-wide experience can be most welcome. For instance, the whole process of learning for an African child must be transposed into African terms. Just as the church gave brilliant leadership in the matter of translating into and out of African languages, so once again she could easily now set up a resource bank of experts to work with the African governments, universities, and UNESCO in translating education. Some of it is still at the level of changing "Johnny's mother bought six apples" to "Kwesi's mother bought six cocoa beans."

Certainly many forms of service in the new African nations are open to the churches, suitable to their experience and resources. While the welfare state is developing, they can pioneer social welfare. As they hand over general hospitals, they may be able to help with psychiatric care, which is all too often at the "snake-pit" stage where the colonial governments left it.

On the coming of independence and during the next few years, African Islam has become more self-consciously aware of what has been achieved and the problems ahead. Islam has been transplanted successfully from North Africa (triumphantly held for Islam) and Arabia to most of the area south of the desert and the savannah as far as, roughly, ten degrees north. There are great areas south of this, such as southwestern Nigeria and northern Cameroon, where Islam is present in strength. In East Africa a belt of Islam stretches from Somalia southward along the coast across Kenya and Tanzania to Mozambique. Inland, in parts of northeast Congo, Uganda, and Malawi, there are considerable pockets of Muslims. Even in South Africa, where Islam goes back to the good Sheikh Yusuf of Bantam, who was deported thither by the Dutch, and has been the religion of underprivileged slaves, exiles, and Asian immigrants, this religion is spreading. In fact statistics, where they are available, indicate that the number of Muslims is multiplying both by natural increase (for most Muslims rejoice in numerous children and care little for artificial birth control) and by conversion. In addition to general numbers, Muslims of the highest quality both in piety and learning are not scarce. Muslim influence is formidable: in Algeria, Tunisia, and Egypt it pervades every facet of life, and though governments may bring in all kinds of innovations, they have to take Islam most carefully into account. In Morocco there is a Muslim monarchy. Mauretania has declared herself a Muslim republic. In the Sudan official rule is in the hands of the northerners, who are Muslim. In Senegal the Muslim lobby is powerful; Islam, based on the preponderant north, has a great voice in

Nigerian affairs, while in Somalia it is bound up with the very notion of nationhood.

After bitter experience of what religion can do in politics, the concept of the separation of religion and the state has been adopted in many Western countries. There are African Muslims who say this is one of the main reasons why open sin and crime abound in those very countries. In Islam the issues are much more complicated. A learned Uganda sheikh explained that the Apostle of God in his own lifetime set up an Islamic state, and rule on God's behalf was vested in the *umma,* the Muslim community, and those whom they chose. (This is the Sunni view, and very few Muslims in Africa are not Sunni.) In a country ruled by non-Muslims or by people who claim to be Muslim but are not really so, the Muslims live in obedience to the government as long as nothing flagrantly opposed to Islam is carried out. If this comes about they have the right to withdraw to the nearest properly Muslim area.

In a debate about this, young Uganda Muslim students cited the case of India. In 1947 Muslims felt that they had to have somewhere where they ruled and could build up an Islamic state. Most of them hived off to form Pakistan, but what of the eighty million or so left to live among Hindus? Nowadays a Muslim must be concerned to build up his nation, that is his Islamic duty.

A long series of interviews in Ghana, Nigeria, Uganda, Kenya, and Tanzania would indicate that this younger generation of (Western-) educated Muslims in anglophone Africa concentrates on the problem of modernization in a way reminiscent of the Turks and the Middle East of recent generations. They maintain courtesy and public respect for the "greybeards." They would like to see the Muslims much more concerned to make full use of modern education, especially science and modern medicine. They feel medieval Arab medicine was fine in its day, but it is just ridiculous to see people still searching in musty old tomes for cures and old wives' recipes. Rich men, instead of looking to themselves by flying in luxury on the *hajj* and staying in expensive hotels, should send promising students on scholarships wherever training is available.

These young people frequently say that in their opinion Islam in the different African countries should set up central organizations and secretariats of the kind the government and the churches have. There should be more international contacts with Muslim countries such as Pakistan and Saudi Arabia. Steps should be taken to prevent the kind of factionalism—based on tribalism and the cult of personalities—which has so violently torn Muslims apart in places like Uganda and southwestern Nigeria for years on end. And these organizations are, in fact, gathering strength. As we saw above, His Highness the late Aga Khan started the East African Muslim Welfare Society. His grandson has continued the tradition with visits, generous gifts, and constant support.

Their thinking on the evolution of Islam in the modern world has had considerable influence in East Africa and Pakistan. Muslims should use all kinds of modern expert knowledge and live as full members of the modern world while maintaining their Islamic quality by renewed attention to the basics of their religion, which are few and not difficult to keep. In Uganda in recent years the nation-wide National Association for the Advancement of Muslims has been set up amidst bitter recriminations from the community around Kibuli mosque at Kampala, who considered that the older organization, far from representing only Ganda Muslims, spoke for all Uganda Muslims. It may be some years before the matter is sorted out, but there is little fear that Islam will cease to prosper and spread.

As for international contacts and a secretariat, Africans going on the pilgrimage are being invited to various pan-Islamic and Islamic ecumenical conferences and are being placed on international committees. The financial backing for these ventures is mainly from Kuwait, Saudi Arabia, and Pakistan. The great promise of some of these movements has already been dashed by the unscrupulous way in which certain politicians have used them for their own purposes and international religious causes have been hitched to the chariots of certain rather minor nations.

It is not easy to obtain a representative sample of what modern young African educated Muslim women are thinking, since not very many of them have been getting into the upper forms of secondary schools and the university. It has been clear since Ibn Battuta's day at least that African women will maintain a position of prominence, freedom, and independent action. The Muslim women students interviewed over a period of years in Ghana, Nigeria, and East Africa were every one proud of their Islam. They did not feel that Islam gave them a position of subjection, but rather that it recognized and honored them as women. Naturally their duty when married would be to care for their husband and children. They did not fear that their husbands would take an additional wife or two—economic circumstances and modern conditions in general made that unlikely. As for pursuing a career, this was not more difficult for them than for other modern women who were wives and mothers. They pointed out that they realized their fortunate position as many Muslims, especially in the country districts, lagged behind. They would have to do all they could to help them. This may seem rather a rosy picture, but one may suppose that a woman investigator, preferably a grandmother, who would spend some years making friends on the basis of common womanly interests, would bring in a similar picture, based on broader evidence.

Christianity and Islam are sister religions, and in their relationship to one another somewhat ugly sisters. In tropical Africa Muslims have, as a whole, managed to measure up well to the high standard in this matter laid down by their religion. They respect Christians as "people of the Book" and pay due reverence to Jesus as a prophet and to his mother. They have bitterly resented the discrimination and third-class-citizen status they have been made to feel by some Christians. They have looked with contempt on the behavior of some Christian missionaries. There was a time, for instance, when in Ghana or Uganda the only way for a Muslim to get his son a higher education was to send him to a Christian school. Then the people there would go out of their way to convert him. Or, again, if your wife was ill and you sent her to a mission hospital, they would take advantage of her illness to preach the gospel to her. "When you are bleeding down below do you jump out of bed and run away?" one of them asked.

On the Christian side, the general level of approach to Islam has fallen far below the standards set by St. Francis and Raymond Lull in the middle ages. In Victorian times Christian thinking was dominated by the kind of controversies which had been carried on in India. Alongside a display of Islamic learning, attacks were made on the personal life of the Prophet and other insulting lines of argument pursued. The high standard of the learning is evidenced by the fact that Mohammed Ashraf of Pakistan has republished Hughes' *Diction-*

ary of Islam which appeared in 1885 (with careful deletion of nastinesses). The other standard work regularly available to Christians and much older was Pfander's *Mizan ul Haqq,* with a veritable battery of weapons to hurl at Muslim heads. Rich amends were made by people such as H. U. Weitbrecht Stanton, who did so much to civilize the training of young missionaries going to Muslim countries; Temple Gairdner, who worked in Egypt; Canon Dale in Zanzibar, and Kenneth Cragg, who made long journeys through Africa and now lives in the Middle East. Samuel Zwemer did a similar work in the U.S.A. These men tried to keep the controversy clean, and they emphasized the many basic features the two religions have in common. They did not minimize the differences, and were careful to point out that they did not believe all religions are merely expressions of the same thing.

On the Catholic side, too, a constructive approach to Islam has for some time been the order of the day. The White Fathers have always paid special attention to Islam and recall that it was a Muslim who persuaded Kabaka Mutesa to let them begin work in Uganda (in contrast, Christians may note with shame, to Mackay's Protestant denunciations). The Jesuits and Franciscans have also sought to approach Islam by means of honest and deep study. We must remember also the life and work of Charles de Foucauld, who studied and served the Tuareg, living amongst them till he was killed in 1916. (Knowing what we do today of the use military men can make of any innocently collected information, and what French and Italian imperialists did in the Sahara, the killing of the father should cause less surprise than his being spared so long.) In recent years the work of the monks of Toumlilene to bring together Muslims and Christians in residential conferences, unconsciously but effectively paralleled by the extramural and extension departments of the universities in Ghana and Uganda, has led to the build-up of mutual understanding.

Today, on the whole, Christians and Muslims accept each other as permanent features of the African landscape. Their leaders are careful to exchange official courtesies and show each other every kind of respect. The African rank and file will often join in the singing of Christmas carols, and in due course honor the birthday of the Prophet at a *maulidi.* They will make a pomp out of a circumcision or a baptism; a Muslim bride will appear at her wedding in white and receive a ring (this is not to imply that either is specifically Christian). The followers of the two religions can be friendly in this way and yet avoid confusion over essentials.

The Arabness of Islam is a kind of carapace or shell which can give her strength to do her work and be herself wherever she goes. To Christianity her Europeanness is *impedimenta,* luggage she has picked up which may or may not be useful. Often it is best to lose it and collect a new lot where you are. Both religions have achieved so much, going forward in the way of God, both have gone through immigrant and resident alien status and become citizens. There is at Edinburgh a fourteenth-century Muslim illuminated manuscript which shows the Prophet Muhammad riding on a war-camel conversing with Jesus riding on an ass. For the last eighty years or so their roles have been reversed in Africa; Christianity came in with conquerors and Islam came in meek and lowly. They have each had their due reward. Islam as a whole is free of the stigma attached to the slave trade and the wars which certain Muslims carried on to up to less than a century ago. She has regained international contact and the prestige of a world religion. She stands as firm as a rock. The revolution Islam brings to individuals and societies will take place. When, in a century from now, all this talk about modernization and mixing of religion has died away, she will be stronger than ever.

The love affair between Christ and the church on the African continent goes back two millennia. At the present time the church has a future and possibilities more dazzling than anything we can imagine, if only she can dissociate herself from some of the misdeeds of her rascally self-appointed friends of the past (and of the present in southern Africa). Perhaps at last we may be allowed to discern her as she really is, in all her beauty, black and comely and arrayed as a bride for her Lord.

Here we must leave stringing together this small garland of flowers, leaves, and grasses. May God who knows the truth about the whole proceedings, in his compassion and mercy, forgive that which is lacking and that which misses the mark.

Do-It-Yourself Notes, Sources, and Reading List

In this guide we give only those books found directly useful to faculty and students in seminars, field visits, workshops, and lectures. In many cases there are much better books which we did not know about or could not obtain. A number of other books used in research or preparation have not been named, but the titles of most of these are recoverable by those who want to go deeper by using the works mentioned.

General background

Students find it useful to read such books as R. Oliver and J. D. Fage: *A Short History of Africa* (Penguin, 2nd ed., 1966); R. Cornevin: *Histoire de l'Afrique* (Paris, 1962; paperback ed., Port Washington, N.Y., 1970); Basil Davidson: *Africa, History of a Continent* (London and New York, 1966), and refer to their suggestions for further reading. Both John Mbiti's *African Religions and Philosophies* (London and New York, 1969) and Geoffrey Parrinder's Penguin *Religion in Africa* (1969) have sections on Christianity and Islam and bibliographies. Ernst Dammann: *Die Religionen Afrikas* (Stuttgart, 1963), is especially good on the fundamental German work on both Christianity and Islam in Africa. Eds. John N. Paden and Edward W. Soja: *The African Experience,* vol. 1—*Essays* (Evanston, 1970), gives a helpful overall survey —and volume 11—*Bibliographic References* (1968)—is especially valuable for its coverage of articles in periodicals. The booklist given in Noel Q. King:

Religions of Africa (New York, 1970), mentions selected books which give basic geographical, anthropological, and linguistic background material. J. D. Fage: *An Atlas of African History* (Cambridge and New York, 1963), is a constant companion.

Two of the major regions of Africa are particularly well served by readily available books. On West Africa see J. F. A. Ajayi and I. Espie: *A Thousand Years of West African History* (Ibadan, London, and New York, 1965), and J. D. Fage: *A History of West Africa* (Cambridge and New York, 4th ed. 1969). Virginia Thompson and Richard Adloff's: *French West Africa* (London, 1958), gives an excellent general background and has a section on Christianity, Fetishism (*sic*), and Islam in the period before 1939. On East Africa see R. Oliver and Gervase Mathew: *History of East Africa,* volume I (Oxford and New York, 1963). The second volume was edited by Vincent Harlow and E. M. Chilvers, and published in 1965. A third volume edited by D. A. Low and John Lonsdale is awaited.

A beginner or someone doing only a quarter or two's study would do well to concentrate on these two regions and later go on to others. For guidance with regard to the others, see Roland Oliver and Anthony Atmore: *Africa since 1800* (Cambridge and New York, 1967). J. C. Anene and Godfrey Brown: *Africa in the Nineteenth and Twentieth Centuries* (London, 1966), is of great value to teachers. Robert I. Rotberg's *A Political History of Tropical Africa* (New York, 1965), is a stimulating guide.

Christianity in Africa is blessed/cursed with mammoth tomes. The first is K. S. Latourette: *The History of the Expansion of Christianity* which deals with Africa in volume III— *Three Centuries of Advance, 1500–1800* (London and New York, no date on 1st ed.); volume V— *The Great Century, 1800– 1914, The Americas, Australasia and Africa* (1943); vol. VI— *The Great Century, Northern Africa and Asia*, no date on 1st ed.; vol. VII— *Advance Through Storm, 1914 and After* (1945). The second is C. P. Groves: *The Planting of Christianity in Africa* (London and New York, four volumes, 1st ed. 1948– 1958, reissued 1964). Both are indispensable reference compilations. They take the mission society approach: "In year x, Society y sent Reverend z to open station a." It has been discovered that in places the separate paragraphs can be read in inverse order without seriously dislocating the solid onward flow of facts marshaled in log-jam order under years and areas. Both authors believe that the African earth will be eventually filled with the glory of God. The enormous recessions of Christianity in the eighth and eighteenth centuries are washed under a wave theory; the third wave—the modern one—will presumably carry all before it. At the same time Groves will remain the Eusebius of African church history for some time. He was the first to find his way through the thicket and others must follow those paths. For the background of the African missions in the world mission of Christianity, see Stephen Neill's *A History of Christian Missions* (Pelican, 1964); the rest of Latourette's seven-volume *Expansion* and H-W. Gensichen: *Missionsgeschichte der neueren Zeit* (Goettingen, 1961). Schools of African historians (as against historians of Africa) are emerging in Senegal, Nigeria, Uganda, Kenya, and Tanzania among other places. So far even fewer African church historians (as against African historians dealing with the church or church historians dealing with Africa) have emerged. Some idea of the situation in 1965 can be gained from ed. C. G. Baeta: *Christianity in Tropical Africa* (London and New York, 1968). The articles themselves and the books cited in the footnotes are a valuable onward guide to students who have already gotten a grasp of the subject.

Islam in Africa has not yet had the benefit of successful large-scale work in English by a Muslim. India-Pakistan and Egypt were our best hope but Mahmud Brelvi: *Islam in Africa* (Lahore, 1964), becomes a kind of handbook to the continent (a task brilliantly fulfilled by Colin Legum), so that one hesitates to mention it for our purpose. Various works in Arabic by Egyptians are inaccessible to the outside world but it is to be hoped they will be made available in translation. For instance, during an unexpected short visit to a Cairo bookstore the writer hurriedly and perhaps inaccurately noted from the Arabic—H. I. Hassan: *Islam and Arabic Culture* (education?) *in Africa* (Cairo, 1963).

The monument of inspired compilation on the Islamic side corresponding to Groves' *Planting of Christianity* is J. Spencer Trimingham's volumes— *Islam in the Sudan* (Oxford and New York, 1949; reprinted 1965), *Islam in Ethiopia* (Oxford and New York, 1952; reprinted 1965), *Islam in West Africa* (Oxford and New York, 1959), *A History of Islam in West Africa* (Oxford and New York, 1962), *Islam in East Africa* (Oxford and New York, 1964), and *The Influence of Islam upon Africa* (London and New York, 1968.) Trimingham is a Christian missionary and a university professor of the type who is saturated with his subject of study and tries to be scrupulously academically honest in his treatment of it. Total objectivity is neither possible nor desirable. If one knows a person's standpoint one can allow for it. Some African Muslims in the Western tradition appreciate his work as a Christian service to Islam—like Ibn Battuta describing Christian Constantinople in the fourteenth century. Others see it as the combination of white man and missionary extending paternalism and colonialism into the field of scholarship. J. N. D. Anderson's *Islamic Law in Africa* (London, 1954 and reprinted), is in a similar category. We may now add Nehemia Levtzion: *Muslims and Chiefs in West Africa* (Oxford and New York, 1968) to this list. It is probable that other contributions by Israeli scholars will be forthcoming, for instance Arye

Oded has done some fundamental research on Islam in Buganda. T. W. Arnold: *The Preaching of Islam* (republished at Lahore in 1961) is old and in trying to be fair to Islam tends to overcompensate, but is still useful.

The papers presented at the Fifth International African Seminar (at Zaria in 1964) were edited by I. M. Lewis as *Islam in Tropical Africa* (Oxford and New York, 1966). Each theme has an extensive bibliography. An important American contribution which brings together an international team of scholars (including one Muslim) is James Kritzeck and William H. Lewis: *Islam in Africa* (New York and London, 1969). The bibliographical work is most helpful. A few of the chapters are regrettably weak.

Writers in French such as Paul Marty and Alphonse Gouilly have done monumental work on Islam in former French Africa. Full bibliographies will be found in J. C. Froelich: *Les musulmans d'Afrique noire* (Paris, 1962), and Vincent Monteil: *L'Islam noir* (Paris, 1964).

Useful reference work on Islam in which students can hunt both people and things include: ed. H. A. R. Gibb and J. H. Kramers: *Shorter Encyclopaedia of Islam* (Leiden, London, and Ithaca, reprinted 1961), and T. P. Hughes: *A Dictionary of Islam* (reprinted at Lahore, 1964; in U.S.A., Clifton, N.J.). For background see Alfred Guillaume's Penguin *Islam* (1954 and reprinted), H. A. R. Gibb's *Mohammedanism* (Oxford and New York, 2nd ed., 1953, and reprinted), and Bernard Lewis' *The Arabs in History* (Harper Torchbook revision, 1966). W. Montgomery Watt publishes a new handbook on an Islamic theme most years. His *Muhammad, Prophet and Statesman* (Oxford and New York, 1961), is an excellent guide to the life of the Prophet. Kenneth Cragg's profound and lyrical understanding of Islam is best represented by his *Call of the Minaret* (Oxford and New York, 1956, reissued since), or *Sandals at the Mosque* (London and Naperville, 1959). On Muslim law see Joseph Schacht: *An Introduction to Islamic Law* (Oxford and New York, 1964).

Oral sources and audio-visual aids. Africans able to communicate with regard to their own traditions and religion are to be found in most parts of the world and of course are to be approached with courtesy and respect. They are often our best source. A study-visit to Africa after careful planning, so as not to become a nuisance, is a real possibility, especially if one can join in with an organization like Crossroads Africa or such field-programs as that of Kalamazoo or of the University of California.

On the *music, dance, and recordings* side, to the entries in King's *Religions of Africa,* pp. 101–103, add: Fred Warren: *The Music of Africa* (New York, 1970), B. A. Arning: *An Annotated Bibliography of Music and Dance in English-speaking Africa* (Legon, Ghana, 1967), and African Bibliographic Center: *"The Beat Goes On," a Selected Guide to Resources on African Music and Dance 1965–1967* (Washington, D.C. 1968). *Phase two—a supplementary guide,* by the same center, appeared in 1969.

Recordings by various groups easily accessible to students continue to be reissued or become available. For instance in *la collection musée de l'homme,* the disc *musique d'Afrique occidentale* (1968), the Folkways *Music from Tunisia,* the Afrotone *Music from the Sudan,* UNESCO *Music of Kanem* and *The Music of Ethiopia—the Ethiopian Church* are all relevant to our theme. The Asch Mankind Series is a new venture. Their *Ewe Music of Ghana* is from Anyako where Christianity and Ewe Traditional Religion had a clash. Their *Music of the Idoma* gives us some of the funeral chants of that interesting people who live on the Benue river some hundred miles above the confluence. The student can spend many a rewarding hour poking around catalogs and *discotheques.*

On *films and video-tapes* the best place to start looking is in the catalogs of the Audio-Visual and African Centers of Universities such as Boston, Indiana, and U.C.L.A., under such headings as "Religion," "Africa," "Christianity", and "Islam." Gems relevant to our purpose will be unearthed, such as the N.E.T. *Religions of Mankind,* "Christianity" and "Islam" and "African Village Life in Mali." The latter title disguises the annual commemoration of the ancestors and various rites of divination among the Dogon. It is fair to warn anyone who sees them and rereads Marcel Griaule's *Conversations with Ogotemmeli* (London and New York, 1965) that he will talk of nothing else till his friends will refer to him as "that doggone Dogon."

Embassies will loan films. Thus the Senegalese *Barom Sarret* is a brilliant study in the life of a Dakar carter with Islam, traditional beliefs and the cathedral peeping in. Egypt (U.A.R.) lends films on such diverse topics as St. Catherine's monastery and a thousand-minareted visit to Cairo.

Resource material in the way of *slides and film strips* is abundant. Most headquarters of church groups and missions have visual aids depicting "their" Christians. Slide shows can be made up by copying photos out of books, seeking out the collections of retired missionaries, combing slide libraries. The best this writer has seen is obtainable from the Audio-Visual Aids Centre, Makerere University, P. O. Box 7062, Kampala, Uganda.

Collections of documents. The following have been found helpful: B. Davidson: *The African Past* (Penguin, 1964), G. S. P. Freeman-Grenville: *The East African Coast* (1962). Anyone who delights in poking about in obscure parts of libraries and bookstores will enjoy (only partially directed) serendipities which befell our students such as the following: (i) The Penguin Eusebius: *History of the Church* has much to say on the church in Egypt. (ii) *Patrologia Orientalis,* vol. V—History of the [Alexandrian] Patriarchs, Arabic and English in parallel, ed. B. T. A. Evetts. (iii) Migne's *Patrologia Latina,* vol. XXI, col. 478 ff. give Rufinus: *Historia Ecclesiastica* X 9—Christianity comes to

Ethiopia. (iv) *Graeci Inscriptiones Selectae,* ed. Dittenberger, vol. I, p. 303—Inscription in Greek by Silko, Kinglet of the Nobadae and Ethiopians from the temple at Kalabshah—how God gave him the victory over idol-worshipers. (Perhaps relates to the conversion of Nubia.) (v) "The Third Part of the Ecclesiastical History of John of Ephesus," Bk. IV, translated by Payne Smith (Oxford, 1860), contains the account of the conversion of Nubia given in the text. (vi) Pope Gregory to his missionaries in England telling them to be gentle with the filthy habits of the local savages, *Patrologia Latina* CXIX, Col. 877 f. Also in the Penguin Bede: *A History of the English Church and People,* pp. 71 ff. (vii) The *Hakluyt Voyages* series are an unending source of discovery—Leo Africanus (Hasan Ibn Muhammad al Wazzan al Zayyati after being baptized by the pope wrote an account of his travels in Africa as far as Gobir, Katsina, and Kano), three volumes, ed. R. Brown (1896). Francisco Alvarez: *The Prester John of the Indies,* ed. C. F. Beckingham and G. W. B. Huntingford, two volumes (1961). The same scholars edited M. de Almeida: *Some Records of Ethiopia* (1593–1646), 1954.

Some students in Uganda and Ghana began successfully to hunt manuscripts, typescripts, and pamphlets. Once a volume of a handwritten history in Luganda was brought in on the same day as a Persian recipe for turning copper into gold.

There is a large and interesting literature in such languages as Twi, Ewe, Yoruba, Ibo, Hausa, Luganda, and Swahili. The last is the one which pays the richest and quickest dividends. Contemporary writings by missionaries and government officials in English, French, and Portuguese go back over a couple of centuries and often make exciting reading. David Livingstone's *Missionary Travels and Researches* (New York and London, 1858), and his *Last Journals* (1875), are masterpieces of their kind. Only a Victorian could have commented, after a lifetime of solitary wandering, on Jesus' pronouncement: "Lo, I am with you even to the end of the world," with the remark: "It is the word of a gentleman of the very strictest honor." Other examples of this literature are: by an American, T. J. Bowen: *Adventures and Missionary Labors in Africa, 1849 to 1856* (reprinted in 1968 and published in London and Westport, Conn., with an introduction by Dr. E. A. Ayandele, an African professor whose first schools were run by Bowen's mission); by a German, J. Ludwig Krapf: *Travels, Research and Missionary Labors* (1860; reprinted London and New York, 1968).

Prominent in the category of original documents come *novels and poetry by African writers.* Probably the novels of Chinua Achebe are our best guide to the process of "pacification," colonial modernization, the looking for freedom and the bitterness of finding that it does not automatically bring paradise but demands a new kind of human. The following should be read: *Things Fall Apart* (1958), *No Longer at Ease* (1960), *Arrow of God* (1964), and *A Man of the People* (1966). Achebe is from eastern Nigeria and went through the tragedy of Biafra.

The plays and poems of Wole Soyinka of Yorubaland can be followed up in the *Three Crowns* series published by Oxford. Many of them have delightful sideswipes at religion together with a basic permeation by it. Amos Tutuola's novels teach us more about the survival of A.T.R. in modern Africa than a textbook could. Films regarding these authors and a number of African thinkers are available.

Kwesi Armah's *The Beautyful Ones Are Not Yet Born* (Boston and New York, 1968) gives an incredibly palpable picture of Ghana in the last years of Dr. Nkrumah's regime. William Conton's novels on Sierra Leone reveal a deep understanding of human nature and the part religion plays in it.

There is a tremendous literature in French by Africans, ranging from the political and philosophical outpourings of Leopold Senghor to the bittersweet humor of Ferdinand Oyono. (On Senghor see the selection and translation by John Reed and Clive Wake [Oxford, 1965]. On Oyono see *The Old Man and the Medal* or *Houseboy.*) A fair amount of it has been translated into English. Cheikh Hamidou Kane's *Ambiguous Adventure* (London and New York, 1969) is a brilliant account of a young Muslim from Qur'an school entering the Western world.

On the East African side some novels by writers like Grace Ogot and David Rubadiri are useful for our purpose. See also the novels of James Ngugi: *Weep Not Child* (London, 1964); *The River Between* (1965); *A Grain of Wheat* (1967), *The Black Hermit* (1968). Okot p'Bitek's *Song of Lawino* (Nairobi, 1966) is as pungent as a *Lament* played on bagpipes. The reader wonders how so "ridiculous" a performance can bring the tears to his eyes.

English literature written by Black South Africans has already a venerable record. Thomas Mfolo's *Chaka* seems to sum up the Zulu tragedy as the Faust or *Goetterdaemmerung* myth sums up that of the white man. Chaka lies with Noliwe, the only person besides his mother, Nandi, that he has every really loved, then he kills her (she understands and tacitly accepts) and hands her body to his sorcerers so that they may preserve the power of his kingdom. He also kills Nandi. Some more recent works, being born in human agony like Second Isaiah or the Spirituals, reach similar heights. A reliable guide to the literature so far as it goes is J. A. Ramsaran: *New Approaches to African Literature* (London, Ibadan, and New York, 1965).

Chapter One

Christianity first comes to Africa. Standard works on the early church as a whole such as Henry Chadwick: *The Early Church* (Pelican, 1967), have sections on the church in Egypt and North Africa, seeing the story from the point of view of a Mediterranean-centered church. *Early African Christianity,* ed. J. B. Webster and Obaro Ikime as vol. 2, no. 1 (1967) of *Tarikh,* the journal of the Historical Society of Nigeria (Longmans and Humanities Press), uses the African-centered approach.

A great deal can be learned through the biographical approach, looking up the main people and societies named in our text in F. L. Cross: *The Oxford Dictionary of the Christian Church* (Oxford, 1957), or the forthcoming ed. Stephen Neill: *Concise Dictionary of the Christian World Mission,* or his *History of Christian Missions* (Pelican, 1964), The translations and paraphrases from Greek and Latin are by the author, who is glad to acknowledge the help of J. W. T. Allen in revising them.

The Egyptian Church. B. T. A. Evetts and A. J. Butler: *Churches and Monasteries of Egypt and some neighboring countries, attributed to Abu Salih* (Oxford, 1895), chapters in ed. S. R. K. Glanville: *The Legacy of Egypt (Oxford, 1942).* E. R. Hardy: *Christian Egypt* (New York, 1952). A. S. Atiya: *A History of Eastern Christianity* (London and Notre Dame, 1968). Edward Wakin: *A Lonely Minority* (New York, 1963). K. Wessel: *Coptic Art* (London and New York, 1965).

The churches of Roman Africa. W. H. C. Frend: *The Donatist Church* (Oxford, 1952). Tertullian, Cyprian and Augustine in the Loeb Classical Library or translations like the pre-Nicene Fathers (reprinted at Grand Rapids) or the Ancient Christian Writers Series (London and Baltimore). Robert Graves' *Count Belisarius* gives us a glimpse of conditions during the East Roman *reconquista* from the Vandals. John Cooley's *Baal, Christ, and Mohamed, Religion and Revolution in North Africa* (New York, 1965) brings the story of religion in that area right up to modern times. The story of Hadrian the African will be found in Bede's *History* IV 1 and V 20, 23.

The Nubian churches. A. J. Arkell: *A History of the Sudan* (London, 2nd ed., 1961). U. Monneret de Villard: *Storia della Nubia Christiana* (Rome, 1938). P. L. Shinnie: *Mediaeval Nubia* (Khartoum, 1954). P. L. Shinnie: "New Light on Medieval Nubia," *Journal of African History,* VI, 3 (1965), pp. 263–273. Kazimierz Michalowski: "La Nubie chrétienne," *Africana Bulletin* (Warsaw, 1965), 111, pp. 9–25. K. Michalowski: *Faras, die Kathedrale aus dem Wuestensand* (Zurich, 1967). A series of articles in *Kush* and the *Journal of Egyptian Archaeology* from 1960 onward is worth following. The writer is obliged to Professor Shinnie for his patience with him in talking over many archaeological matters to do with Nubia and to Rabbi Posen for going over the Syriac of John of Ephesus with him.

The Ethiopian church. J. Doresse: *Ethiopia* (London and New York, 1956). "The Glorious Victories of Amda Seyon" translated by Huntingford (Oxford,

1966), about incidents in the year 1329. A. H. M. Jones and Elisabeth Munroe: *A History of Ethiopia* (Oxford, 1935; reissued 1966). E. Ullendorf: *The Ethiopians* (London, 1965). C. Jesman: *The Ethiopian Paradox* (London and New York, 1963).

Chapter Two

Islam across the Sahara: The writings of a number of *Muslim Geographers, Travelers, and Historians* are available to Western readers. The text of the *Voyages of Ibn Battuta* used was that of C. Defremery and R. Sanguinetti, 4 volumes (Paris, 1843–58). The writer is indebted to Said Hamdun, who is now a Reader in the University at Nairobi, for the privilege of going over the Arabic word by word with him. A translation with notes of the Black African section of the *Travels* was published at Dakar in 1966 by Mauny, Monteil, and others. H. A. R. Gibb published two volumes of a translation with notes in the Hakluyt series which include the East African section. It is hoped that the third and fourth (with the West African travels) will appear soon. In the meantime his *Selections* published in 1929 are most helpful. It is interesting to compare Ibn Battuta's *Voyages* with the *Travels* of Marco Polo (Penguin, 1958) though unfortunately the Christian did not get to Black Africa.

Many volumes on Ibn Khaldun are available. Probably M. Mahdi: *Ibn Khaldun's Philosophy of History* (Chicago, 1964), and N. J. Dawood's abridgment of Rosenthal's translation of the *Muqaddimah* (New York and London, 1967), would suffice a student desiring to look for himself.

U.N.E.S.C.O. has been republishing some older works with French and Arabic in the same book, such as es-Sadi: *Tarikh es-Soudan* (Paris, 1964) and Mahmud al-Kati: *Tarikh al-Fattash* (Paris, 1964). This is a signal service to religious studies, though the general policy of the organization has been to exclude religion. It is recognized as an essential part of social and cultural life but is presumably too hot and troublesome to handle.

On the romance of *the old Sahara* perhaps there will be time to read only E. W. Bovill: *Caravans of the Old Sahara* (London, 1933). (*The Golden Trade of the Moors,* 2nd ed. [Oxford and New York, 1970], is a version of this.) Adu Boahen's *Britain, the Sahara and the Western Sudan,* 1788–1861 (Oxford, 1964), covers the later part of the story but looks a long way back as well.

On Islam in the middle Volta area see N. Levtzion: *Muslims and Chiefs in West Africa* (Oxford and New York, 1968). Anyone wishing to do a detailed armchair study of the penetration of Islam into a tribal society will enjoy the story of Islam among the Gonja and Dagomba peoples in Northern Ghana. There are local sources, "drum-histories," "enskinment-traditions," and accession lists. J. A. Braimah and J. Goody: *Salaga, the Struggle for Power*

(Oxford and New York, 1967) is a good place to begin.
About Islam in East Africa at this time see P. S. Garlake: *Early Islamic Architecture on the East African Coast* (Oxford, 1966); G. S. P. Freeman-Grenville: *The Medieval History of the Coast of Tanganyika* (Oxford and New York, 1962), and his article "Islam and Christianity in East Africa before the mid-nineteenth century," *African Ecclesiastical Review,* II (1960), pp. 193–207. See also J. S. Kirkman: *Men and Monuments of the East African Coast* (London, 1964).
For a detailed history of a Muslim *tariqa* see Jamil M. Abun-Nasr: *The Tijaniyya* (Oxford and New York, 1965). For a classic of English prose see E. E. Evans-Pritchard: *The Sanusi of Cyrenaica* (Oxford, 1949). On that Muslim order also see N. A. Ziadeh: *Sanusiyah* (Leiden, 1958). On the *city of Timbuktu* see Horace Miner: *Timbuctoo* (New York, rev. ed., 1965).
Christianity's second attempt. Ralph M. Wiltgen's: *Gold Coast Mission History* (Techny, 1956) will be found useful for the detail it gives of one region. There are treatments of other regions too; of these Sir John Gray: *Early Portuguese Missionaries in East Africa* (London, 1958) is the most interesting. W. G. L. Randles: *L'ancien royaume du Congo* (The Hague, 1968) gives a helpful outline of the work there.

Chapter Three

The Slave Trade: P. B. Curtin: *Africa Remembered* (Madison, Wis., 1967); W. Rodney: *West Africa and the Atlantic Slave Trade* (London, Nairobi, and Evanston, 1967); Basil Davidson: *Black Mother* (London and New York, 1961); Daniel P. Mannix and Malcolm Cowley: *Black Cargoes* (New York, 1964); Edward A. Alpers: *The East African Slave Trade* (Nairobi, 1967); J. Duffy: *A Question of Slavery* (Oxford and Cambridge, Mass., 1967); Allan and Humphrey Fisher: *Slavery and Muslim Society in Africa* (London, 1970). Extracts from John Newton's *Journals and Thoughts upon the Slave Trade* were published by Epworth at London in 1962. *Equiano's Travels*—abridged and edited by Paul Edwards (Nairobi and London, 1967). James Mbotela: *Uhuru wa watumwa* (London, 1934; reissued at Nairobi). (It is said a translation into English is to appear.) Abubakar Tafawa Balewa's *Shaihu Umar* (London, 1967) tells the adventures of a man who was enslaved. On *the Chaplains,* see Hans Debrunner: *A History of Christianity in Ghana* (Accra, 1967). On *Dr. Edmund Blyden* see the biography by Hollis Lynch (London and New York, 1966) and his own *Christianity, Islam and the Negro Race* (Edinburgh and Chicago, 1967, being a reprint of the 1887 edition with an introduction by Christopher Fyfe). On Thomas Birch Freeman, see the relevant sections of G. Findlay and W. Holdsworth's account of the Wesleyan

Missionary Society (London, 1921–24), and a recent study by a Swarthmore professor—Harrison Wright in ed. McCall, Bennett, and Butler: *Studies in Western African History* (New York, 1969). On David Livingstone, see the biography by George Seaver (London, 1957). An outstanding biography of Bishop Crowther by a Nigerian scholar is awaited. In the meantime, see Jessie Page: *The Black Bishop* (London, 1908). A precolonial venture not mentioned in the text (into Malawi, there are indeed many others) is gracefully described in Owen Chadwick's *Mackenzie's Grave* (London and Mystic, Conn., 1959).

A student may find it interesting to pursue the history of a given missionary agency in a certain area. He can choose for instance the White Fathers or Society for Missions in Africa (see below the material cited on Catholic work) or such groups as the American Board of Commissioners for Foreign Missions or the Church Missionary Society—using Stephen Neill's forthcoming *Dictionary of the Christian World Mission.* The Church Mission Society was excellently served by three volumes by Eugene Stock which brought its story to 1899. Gordon Hewitt's *The Problems of Success* (London and Naperville, forthcoming) will deal with 1910 to 1942 in tropical Africa and the Middle East. R. Collins and P. Duignan: *Americans in Africa* (Stanford, 1963) is a most useful guide to American archival resources and missionary activities at this time.

Regional or national bibliographies relating to some of the other places mentioned will be found under the notes on Chapters five and six.

Chapter Four

The Fulani *jihad*—H. A. S. Johnston: *The Fulani Empire of Sokoto* (Oxford and New York, 1967), and Murray Last: *The Sokoto Caliphate* (London, 1967), give ample material and bibliography. See also Marilyn R. Waldman: "The Fulani *jihad,* a reassessment," *Journal of African History,* VI (1965), pp. 333–355. For more direct access to sources—H. R. Palmer's *Sudanese Memoirs,* volume III (1928), pp. 105 ff. gives a translation of the *Kano Chronicle.* In the *Journal of the African Society,* vol. XII and XIV, he gives a translation of the Shehu's *Admonition to the Brethren.* A series of articles by Mervin Hiskett in the *Bulletin of the School of Oriental and African Studies* for 1957, 1960, 1962 give original works by the leaders and other information. Heinrich Barth's visit to the Fulani Kingdoms will be found in his *Travels and Discoveries* (London, 1857; reissued, London and New York, 1965), five volumes. Good material for the study of the Pastoral Fulani is available. See Derrick J. Stenning: *Savannah Nomads* (Oxford and New York, 1959) and his pages in ed. James L. Gibbs: *Peoples of Africa* (New York, 1965) and A.

Hampate Ba and G. Dieterlen: *Koumen, texte initiatique des pasteurs peul* (Paris, 1961). On the *Hausa* see D. P. L. Dry: *The Place of Islam in Hausa Society* (unpublished thesis, Oxford, 1952); J. Greenberg: *The Influence of Islam on a Sudanese Religion* (New York, 1946); (translated and ed. F. Heath) Hassan and Shu'aibu: *A Chronicle of Abuja* (Lagos, 1962); Michael Onwuejeogwu: "The cult of the *bori* spirits," in *Man in Africa,* ed. Mary Douglas and P. M. Kaberry (London, 1969), pp. 279 ff.; B. Smith: *Baba of Karo* (London and New York, 1954); M. G. Smith: *Government in Zazzau* (Oxford, 1960), and a section by the same in ed. James L. Gibbs: *Peoples of Africa* (New York, 1965); A. J. N. Tremearne: *Hausa Superstitions and Customs* (London, 1913) and *The Ban of the Bori* (1914). H. A. S. Johnston's *A Selection of Hausa Stories* (Oxford, 1966) is a store of delight. The U.N.E.S.C.O. Anthology of African Music has a record devoted to Hausa music, including Bori. The film *Hausa Village* leads up to a wedding.

The coming of Islam to Nupe which was greatly affected by the *jihad* may be studied in two anthropological classics: S. F. Nadel's *Black Byzantium* (London and New York, 1942) and *Nupe Religion* (London and New York, 1952). Marie-Jose Tubiana's *Survivances preislamiques en pays zaghawa* (Paris, 1964) is a detailed study of the religion of an Islamized group in the Republic of Chad. M. A. Klein's *Islam and Imperialism in Senegal* (New York, 1968) examines in detail the coming of French power and its effect on traditional society and Islam in the Sine-Saloum area not far from the Gambia river, from 1847 to 1914.

The Swahili sources used in this chapter are three. Abdallah bin Hemedi: *Habari za wakilindi* (Nairobi, 1962), translated with notes by J. W. T. Allen (Dar es Salaam, 1963). Secondly, C. Velten: *Desturi za Wasuahili na khabari za desturi za sheria za Wasuaheli* [The customs of the Swahili and information about their legal uses] (Goettingen, 1903), which consists of excerpts from descriptions of customs written down by old men in the 1880's in the Mrima area (that is, the mainland over against Zanzibar island) in Arabic script, transliterated into Roman script. A German translation appeared the same year. Lyndon Harries published selections and their translation in his *Swahili Prose Texts* (Oxford, Nairobi, and New York, 1965). The present writer is working with J. W. T. Allen toward a complete new edition of Velten and translation with notes. Velten's material accurately reflects the situation just before the colonial period and is probably a reliable indication of things from the 1850's onward. An interested student may wish to compare what the *Desturi* say on the *mganga,* on outdooring of babies, on the circumcision camp and the spirit-possession cult with the relevant sections of *Religions of Africa,* to try to gauge the extent to which Islam had penetrated into the African matrix. The third Kiswahili source is the autobiography of Tippu

Tip, edited and translated by W. H. Whiteley (reprinted Nairobi, no date). (The original edition of 1958 and 1959 in the *Journal* of the East African Swahili Committee, if available, is more helpful.)

The description of Islam coming into Uganda is based on a forthcoming work, Abdul Kasozi and Noel King: *Islam and the Confluence of Religions in Uganda.* The old warrior whose words are given was Osmani Wamala who died in 1969 at an age reputedly over 100. Recordings were made in Butambala in September, 1967, by Amin Mutabya, Abdul Kasozi, William Montgomery Watt, and Noel King.

Chapters Five and Six

It is best to arrange the material from here on under selected topics and a few regional or national headings.

Colonialism and the response to it. Only the first volume of L. H. Gann and Peter Duignan: *Colonialism in Africa, 1870-1960* (Cambridge and New York, 1969), has reached the author so far. It deals so thoroughly with the period 1870-1914 that it is likely that with its second and third volumes it will become definitive for a while. The British and French classical expositions will be found in Lugard's *Dual Mandate* (London, 4th ed., 1929, reprinted Hamden, Conn., 1965) and Albert Sarraut's *La mise en valeur des colonies* (Paris, 1941). (Compare also Hubert Deschamps: *"Et maintenant Lord Lugard,"Africa,* XXXII, 4 [1963], pp. 296-306). For an American point of view see Raymond L. Buell: *The Native Problem in Africa* (1st ed., 1928; reprinted Hamden, Conn., 1965). M. A. C. Warren makes some balanced remarks on *the relationship of missions to colonialism* in his *Missionary Movement from Britain in Modern History* (London, 1965). See also Robert Delavignette: *Christianity and Colonialism* (English translation, London and New York, 1964), and Stephen Neill: *Colonialism and Christian Missions* (London and New York, 1966). H. Loth: *Die Christliche Mission in Suedwest Afrika* (Berlin, 1963) is an example of the work done by historians with Marxist tendencies who have access to the old imperial archives in East Germany and have found much about the cooperation of imperialists and missionaries in some former German territories like southwest Africa. This is a healthy development in our study, but obviously our best guides will be trained African historians writing in Africa and even then a central Ugandan or a northern Ghanaian will tell a different story from an Algerian or a Congolese. Kofi Busia's *The Challenge of Africa* (New York, 1962) has a section on colonialism as well as other major problems such as race relations, industrialization, and nationalism. An Indian like R. Desai: *Christianity in Africa as seen by Africans* (Denver, 1962) could have been of great help had he not so obviously collected antimissionary jokes from all over the globe and applied them to Africa and had his selection reflected other African points of view. The following will also be found useful—O. Mannoni: *Prospero and Caliban* (London, 1956); Frantz Fanon: *The Wretched of the Earth* (Penguin, 1967; French original 1961); Albert Memmi: *The Colonizer and the Colonized* (paperback, Boston, 1967; French original 1957); Gustav Jahoda: *White Man* (Oxford, 1961), Helder Camara: *Church and Colonialism* (London and Sydney, 1969 [from Brazil]. Harris W. Mobley: *The Ghanaian's Image of the Missionary, an analysis of the published critiques of Christian missionaries by Ghanaians, 1897-1965* (Leiden, 1970) gives detailed guidance to and extensive quotations of African writers. The history of anticolonial resistance movements with A.T.R. in the ingredients in many parts of Africa is now being widely studied. See A. B. Davidson in edited T. O. Ranger: *Emerging Themes in African History* (Nairobi, 1968). A reader can follow up the golden stool affair in most Ghana history books or in Edwin Smith's *Golden Stool* (London, 1926). (The whole book is a masterful account of the "nearness" of Christianity and the best in African tradition. Smith, Junod, and Roscoe were missionaries whose anthropology is still respected.) The remarks given on Allah–Water and Yakan are based on oral material collected at Arua and Bombo, but see J. H. Middleton: *Lugbara Religion* (London, 1960) and his article in *The Journal of the Royal Anthropological Institute*, XCIII (1963), pp. 96 ff. On *Maji Maji:* Ebrahim Hussein's play *Kinjeketile* is available from Oxford University Press, Nairobi in Swahili and English. It gives a modern East African's views on the revolt. See also J. Iliffe: "The organization of the *Maji Maji* rebellion," *Journal of African History*, VIII, 3, pp. 507 ff., and ed. G. Gwasa and J. Iliffe: *Records of the Maji Maji Rising*, Historical Association of Tanzania, publication IV (Nairobi, 1968). On the Shona-Ndebele revolts see T. O. Ranger in ed. Stokes and Brown: *The Zambesian Past* (Manchester, 1965) and *Revolt in Southern Rhodesia, 1896–1897* (London and Evanston, 1967). There is an extensive literature on *Mau Mau* to which Carl Rosbery and John Nottingham's *Myth of Mau Mau* (New York, 1966), can act as an introduction as long as the reader remembers that everybody on this topic seems to have an ax to grind.

A.T.R. enters the modern period. On the survival of traditional consultation of the spirit-world see William Bascom: *Ifa Divination* (Bloomington, 1969). Laura Bohanan's *Return to Laughter* (New York, 1964) is an "anthropological novel" about an American woman living with a modern African tribe (the Tiv of Nigeria).

Kingship—the classical example is the Kabakaship of Buganda. See debates leading up to the declaration of a republic in the Uganda Parliament (1966–1967) in the Uganda *Hansard* and Kabaka of Buganda: *Desecration of My*

Kingdom (London, 1967). In other places it has triumphantly survived—see the film and TV cover of the recent enstoolment of the Asantihene. Films of ceremonies connected with the *Oba* of Benin are available from the University of Ibadan, for instance, "Ritual of the Igwe Festival." On A.T.R. surviving in Christianity and Islam see Rencontres internationales de Bouaké: *Les religions Africaines traditionnelles* (Paris, 1965); ed. M. Fortes and A. Dieterlen: *African Systems of Thought* (Oxford, 1965); Vincent Mulago: *Un visage Africain du Christianisme, l'union vitale bantu face à l'unité vitale ecclésiale* (Paris, 1965); and B. A. Paauw: *Bantu Christians and Their Churches* (Oxford and New York, 1968).

Islam in the modern period. Two articles by Joseph Schacht sum up the situation and give many valuable references. They are "Islam in Northern Nigeria," *Studia Islamica,* VIII (Paris, 1957), pp. 123 ff., and "Notes on Islam in East Africa," XXIII (1965), pp. 91 ff. A student wishing to study somewhat further might choose Islam in an area (topological or topical) where a good deal of work has recently been done and concentrate on it. For instance, he or she may choose Islam in African politics, the place of woman in the African Muslim world, recent developments in Hausa Islam (basic bibliography given above) or Islam in East Africa among the Swahili-speaking peoples or among the Baganda. On the Swahili side, in addition to the sources mentioned above see A. H. J. Prins: *The Swahili-speaking Peoples* (London and New York, 1961) for the ethnographical basis. The study can open out from there by looking at publications by J. W. T. Allen and Wilfred Whiteley, at periodicals like *Swahili* and the many publications of the East African Literature Bureau which give Swahili originals with English translation. Also see Jan Knappert's *Traditional Swahili Poetry* (Leiden, 1967); *Swahili Islamic Poetry,* two volumes (Leiden, 1970); and *Myths and Legends of the Swahili* (London, 1970).

On Islam in the Senegal and Wolof areas see a forthcoming monograph by Donal Cruise O'Brien on the Murids, Cheikh Tidiane Sy: *La confrérie sénégalaise des mourides* (Paris, 1969), and Lucy C. Behrmann: *Muslim Brotherhoods and Politics in Senegal* (Cambridge, Mass., 1970). Blaise Senghor did a brilliant film in 1961 on the pilgrimage to Touba of the Murids.

On *Ahmaddiyyah* see the Munir Report, Lahore, 1954, which tells of the riots in which they suffered in Pakistan. The standard work on them in English is Humphrey J. Fisher's *Ahmadiyah, a Study of Contemporary Islam on the West African Coast* (Oxford and New York, 1963). He has also studied various Muslim groups in other parts of West Africa—see his forthcoming contribution in the Cambridge *History of Islam.*

The Ismailis of East Africa produce a copious flow of literature about themselves. The writer is preparing a series of studies on the religious side of their work. Hatimi Amiji's chapter in Kritzeck and Lewis: *Islam in Africa* (New York, 1969), contains a meticulous bibliography.

On the *Christianization of African rites,* on boys' puberty rites at Masasi, see Bishop Vincent Lucas' "The Christian Approach to Non-Christian Customs" in ed. E. R. Morgan: *Essays Catholic and Missionary* (London, 1928); on girls' in northern Zambia, Mabel Shaw: *God's Candlelights* (London, 1932). Edwin W. Smith's *The Christian Mission in Africa* (London, 1926) is a good indication of the way missionary thought was going at the Le Zoute conference of that year. On death-rites, see S. Gyasi Nimako: *The Christian and Funerals* (Cape Coast, 1954). On marriage there is an extensive literature to which the books listed on page 111 of King: *Religions of Africa* are a guide. John M. Robinson: *The Family Apostolate and Africa* (Dublin, 1964) gives a most valuable conspectus of reading matter which includes government and conference reports.

On Christianity becoming indigenous in Africa, Christianity and African Culture W. C. Willoughby: *The Soul of the Bantu* (New York, 1928) reflects the advanced thinking of those days. The major leap made in the next generation is seen in Christian Council of Gold Coast: *Christianity and African Culture* (Accra, 1955) and *Des prêtes noirs s'interrogent* (Paris, 1956). For the thought of the 1960's see Kwesi Dickson and Paul Ellingworth: *Biblical Revelation and African Beliefs* (London, 1969), Bolaji Idowu: *Towards an Indigenous Church* (London and Ibadan, 1965), Harry Sawyerr: *Creative Evangelism* (London, 1968), Harry Sawyerr: *God, Ancestor or Creator* (London, 1970), John Mbiti: *African Concepts of God* (London, 1970), and *The Eschatology of the New Testament in an African Background* (Oxford, forthcoming). See also the bibliographies under countries like Ghana and Uganda. For a background in the similar challenges to Christianity in other parts of the world, see Charles Forman: *Christianity in the non-Western World* (Englewood Cliffs, N. J., 1967), and ed. James P. Cotter: *The Word in the Third World* (Washington, D.C., 1968).

To compare with the Hausa and the coastal Swahili peoples who have become Muslim, it is useful to study the *partial transition of some traditional groups into Christianity.* The Baganda are a prime example—a full bibliography is given under East Africa. But also see J. K. Russell: *Men without God?* (London, 1966) on the Acholi; Eleanor Vandevort: *A Leopard Tamed* on the Nuer (London and New York, 1968); and Sydney G. Williamson: *Akan Religion and the Christian Faith* (Accra, Oxford, and New York, 1965) on the Ashanti, Fante, and some other peoples of Ghana.

The Religions and the Arts. Music—Traditional religious music is still very much alive; its enemy is the transistor which often enough brings in Afro-American material reworked by Europeans but kills local music-making. A number of general and bibliographic works have been mentioned above. For greater detail on the Christian side see Stephen B. G. Mbunga: *Church Law and Bantu Music* (Schoeneck-Beckenried, 1963). (The thirteenth supplement to *Neue Zeitschrift fuer Missionswissenschaft,* a number of the other supplements are also important for the study of the church's problems in Africa.) On the Protestant side, H. Weman: *African Music and the Church in Africa* (Uppsala, 1960) analyzes some bantu music used by African Lutherans. A lively series of articles has appeared in the *African Ecclesiastical Review* on the topic and in various journals devoted to music in Africa. Articles like that of S. G. Williamson on Fante Lyrics in the Methodist Church have appeared in *Africa.* Kobina Nketia and a dynasty of Ewe musicologists in Ghana have done much by actually performing Christian work in the African mode. The work of Graham Hyslop and his African colleagues has been important in Kenya. For a Tanzanian example, see Howard S. Olson's *Tumshangilie mungu* (Makumira, Usa River, 1968). Recordings of the Congolese *Missa Luba* are readily available in Europe and America. Joseph Kyagambiddwa and Aloysius Lugira have done much in this matter in Uganda. The former's *Ten African Religious Hymns* (Munich, 1963) has a helpful foreword. Of course the Ethiopian Church has done church music in the African fashion for over a millennium; the U.N.E.S.C.O. record collection includes some of its chanting and drumming.

On the Muslim side the issues are complicated and little has been published in English dealing directly with the question. In some places African Muslims just go ahead and express their joy in Allah in whatever mode seems most appropriate. In others, such as Uganda, the African musical genius adapts to techniques which use what is known to be permitted. These include chanting and the *matali* drums. The *matali* is like a tambourine and it is said the companions of the Prophet used them. Other Ganda Muslims take them back to Solomon or Tubal. (See also J. Knappert's *A Choice of Flowers, Swahili Love Poems* [London, forthcoming].) Various Kiganda stringed and wind instruments are being brought into Muslim celebrations by analogy with the use of their counterparts in the Maghrib and Egypt.

On religious art see Gaskin's *Bibliography of African Art* (1965), and King: *Religions of Africa,* pp. 100 f. Dr. A. M. Lugira's book on Christian acculturation in Ganda art is on press. Again the Muslim situation is complicated: this is partly because of the prejudice against graven images of man or beast, partly because of the depressing effect on the local artistic market of cheap and tawdry prints and art objects from Europe and Japan. However, there are definite signs in Hausaland and in parts of Tanzania that an art genuinely Muslim and African is emerging.

On the theater—passion plays and historical pageants abound in African

Christianity and photographic and other records of them get into print. A.T.R. is most definitely theatrogenic in Yorubaland as the old religion was for the Greeks. Fortunately this influence is creeping into Christian drama too. A book on the subject is badly needed. There is no reason why the no-godders should have the best pictures, tunes, and plays.

"Independent," "Separatist," "Rebel" churches. Robert Mitchell and Harold Turner: *A Comprehensive Bibliography of Modern African Religious Movements* (Evanston, 1966) suffices by surfeit, but some books stand out as classics or give regional or methodological coverage—C. G. Baeta: *Prophetism in Ghana* (London, 1962); David B. Barrett: *Schism and Renewal in Africa* (Oxford, New York, and Nairobi, 1968); Bengt Sundkler: *Bantu Prophets in South Africa,* rev. ed. (Oxford, 1961, and reprinted); Wole Soyinka: *The Trials of Brother Jero* in *Three Short Plays* (Oxford, 1969); F. B. Welbourn: *East African Rebels* (Oxford and Nairobi, 1961); F. B. Welbourn and B. A. Ogot: *A Place to Feel at Home* (London, 1966); J. B. Webster: *The African Churches among the Yoruba* (Oxford and New York, 1964); R. L. Wishlade: *Sectarianism in Southern Nyasaland* (Oxford, 1965); H. Turner: *African Independent Church,* 2 vols., (Oxford, 1967). George Shepperson and T. Price's: *Independent African* (Edinburgh and Chicago, 1958) falls into a special category. It deals with John Chilembwe, a man from Nyasaland-/Malawi, who visited the U.S.A. and on his return led a rising against the British. Perhaps symbolically, one of the few people killed in cold blood was a Livingstone. American Black influence crops up in many parts of the African independence struggle and much of it has a religious tinge. Shepperson's "Notes on Negro American influence on the emergence of African nationalism," *Journal of African History* I (1960), pp. 299 ff. is a good place to begin digging.

Reform and pressure groups which reach across the denominations should not be ignored just because they are less interesting than those "who will not tarry for any." Little has been written about the Revival Brethren (*Balokole* —"saved ones") since M. A. C. Warren's *Revival* and Stenning's study of them in Ankole (in ed. M. Fortes and G. Dieterlen: *African Systems of Thought* [Oxford, 1965]), but see chapter 6 of Welbourn and Ogot's *A Place to feel at home* and chapter 12 of Welbourn's *East African Christian.* They have so permeated the Protestant churches in Kenya, Uganda, and parts of Tanzania that any student of the church there must foreswear beer and long hair (or mini-skirts and cigarettes) while working among them. It can also be claimed that they have saved the church. On the *manyano* groups among women in South Africa see Mia Brandel-Syrier: *Black Woman in Search of God* (London, 1962).

The church in modern Africa. The spate of books and pamphlets from every

Catholic Episcopal Conference and every National Christian Council, from many a "Free" church as well as from Rome and Geneva, is well worth studying. T. A. Beetham's *Christianity and the New Africa* (London and New York, 1967), Adrian Hastings' *Church and Mission in Modern Africa* (London and the Bronx, 1967), and J. Mullin: *The Catholic Church in Modern Africa* (London and New York, 1965), give a good over-all view and guidance for study to a mass of literature dealing with specific problems.

Some material dealing especially with Catholic Work. Mgr. S. de La Croix: *Histoire universelle des missions catholiques* (Paris, 1958), 4 vols. Norman R. Bennett: *Studies in East African History, the Holy Ghost Missions* (Boston, 1963). J. B. Jordan: *Bishop Shanahan of Southern Nigeria* (Dublin, 1949). J. M. Todd: *African Mission,* (London, 1961). M. J. Bane: *The Popes and Western Africa* (Staten Island, 1968). E. Matheson: *An Enterprise So Perilous* (Dublin, no date). (Other books on the White Fathers include J. Bouniol [1929], David Attwater [1937] and Glenn Kittler [1957].) Alfred de Soras: *Relations de l'église et de l'état dans les pays d'Afrique francophone* (Paris, 1963) is an example of the stranglehold scholastic methods of thinking and arranging material can still use to kill exciting subjects. Ralph E. S. Tanner: *Transition in African Beliefs* (New York, 1967). W. J. Wilson: *The Church in Africa—Christian Mission in a Context of Change, a Seminar* (New York, 1967). (These last two are expensive and should probably be read while browsing in a bookstore.)

Religious leadership. Training for the Christian Ministry is a large topic in its own right. Bengt Sundkler: *The Christian Ministry in Africa* (London, 1960; abridged edition, London and Naperville, 1962), sets out the area for discussion. A series of reports has been drawn up for the Theological Education Fund. A reappraisal at least as agonized as the Protestant one has gone on in Catholic circles—see, for instance, *Priestly Formation in Africa after Vatican II* (Katigondo, 1967). In the meantime in Africa the pastor and his wife, the celibate priest and his hopes, go on with the work with a sense of vocation seldom seen today in America or Britain. Muslims put down much of the church's success, as they see it, to the Christian ministry. There is a definite move for commissioning and systematically training *mallams, walimu,* and sheikhs.

Charismatic leadership of course wells up on every side. The so-called historical churches are fortunately aware that it is their duty to assist with training leadership in the new groups, while not compassing land and sea to make them bigger hypocrites than themselves.

Religion and education. Ed. David G. Scanlon: *Traditions of African Education* (New York, 1964) is a good place to begin, and his *Church, State and Education in Africa* (New York, 1966) good for a follow-up. His *Education in Uganda* (Washington, 1964) is a helpful case study. Of the numerous other useful books one may perhaps pick out ed. R. P. Beaver: *Christianity and African Education* (Grand Rapids, 1966); ed. Brian Holmes: *Educational Policy and the Mission Schools* (London and New York, 1967) has a chapter on Eastern Nigeria and useful comparative material from India. Kofi Busia: *Purposeful Education for Africa* (The Hague and New York, 1968). Reports on education are important; see for instance, ed. L. J. Lewis: *The Phelps-Stokes Reports on Education in Africa* (Oxford, 1962); report of Kinshasa Conference: "Catholic Education in the Service of Africa" (Brazzaville, 1966); report of Salisbury Conference: *Christian Education in Africa* (London, 1963). Reports by U.N.E.S.C.O., colonial, and national governments are well worth seeking out. A number of histories of famous schools and schoolmasters in Africa are appearing—G. P. McGregor: *King's College, Budo* (Nairobi, 1967); W. E. F. Ward: *Fraser of Trinity and Achimota* (Oxford, Accra, and New York, 1965); L. B. Greaves: *Francis Carey of Kenya* (London, 1969).

Social change, especially Religion in the Towns. Paul Abrecht's *The Church in Rapid Social Change* (Garden City, 1961) started an avalance of reports and conferences by World Council of Churches related people. P. C. Lloyd's *Africa in Social Change* (Penguin, 1967) is a good general introduction to the whole subject. See also ed. P. van den Berghe: *Africa, Social Problems of Change and Conflict* (San Francisco, 1965). General surveys of African towns usually include a section on religion; in any case the reports as a whole deserve study. Kofi Busia: *Report on a Social Survey of Sekondi-Takoradi* (London, 1940). Compare D. K. Fiawoo: "Urbanization and Religion in western Ghana," *Sociological Review,* VII (July, 1959), pp. 83–97. Geoffrey Parrinder: *Religion in an African City* (London, 1954) is about *Ibadan.* The impressive *City of Ibadan* (Cambridge, Ibadan, and New York, 1967), ed. P. C. Lloyd, A. L. Mabogunje, and B. Awe, includes sections on A.T.R. and Christianity by Bolaji Idowu and Islam by F. H. el Masri. A. Cohen's *Custom and Politics in Urban Africa* (Berkeley, 1969) is a detailed study of Hausa groups in Yoruba towns with due attention paid to religious factors. *Accra* was surveyed by Ione Acquah. *Kampala* by Southall and Gutkind (*Townsmen in the Making* [Kampala, 1957]). Students from Makerere began a detailed survey of temples, mosques, and churches in Kampala. It is a veritable holy city with religion under every stone.

On *religion and industry in Africa,* see J. Merle Davis: *Modern Industry and the African* (first published 1932; republished New York, 1968). J. V. Taylor and Dorothea Lehmann: *Christians of the Copperbelt* (London, 1961) has been followed up by All Africa Council of Churches teams from Kitwe. The problems of industrialization and urbanization are at their most acute in

South Africa, but unfortunately the experience gained there is not readily accessible.

On *medical work* by religious groups, see Brian O'Brien: *That Good Physician, the life and work of Albert and Catherine Cook* (London, 1962). On Schweitzer there are many adulatory works and films with which one should compare Davidson Nicol: *Africa, a Subjective View* (London and New York, 1964). Maurice King: *Medical Care in Developing Countries* (Oxford and Nairobi, 1966) presents a general survey of the problems and some solutions. On the *psychiatric and psychosomatic side* see M. J. Field: *Search for Security* (London and Evanston, 1960), T. A. Lambo: *African Traditional Beliefs, Concepts of Health and Medical Practice* (Ibadan, 1962), as well as work at Mulago Hospital, Makerere, by Drs. Hebe Welbourn, Bennett, and Jeliffe. The University at Ibadan made a film, "Were Ni, he is a madman," which is well worth seeing. The Indiana University A-V Center distributes "Medicine Men of Africa."

On uhuru and the new ideologies. An interesting approach is through the speeches and autobiographies of the leading African politicians and thinkers of the time. There is a whole collection in the name of Dr. Kwame Nkrumah which ranges from his description of his boyhood to his latest reflections in exile on neo-colonialism. The writer, as one who worked under him for seven years and received good as well as evil at his hands, can only ask students to judge this man's thought for themselves. Among the extensive writings of Leopold Senghor of Senegal a student may choose out *African Socialism,* translated and edited by Mercer Cook (New York, 1959) and "Pierre Teilhard de Chardin et la politique africaine" in *Cahiers de Chardin* III (Paris, 1962), pp. 13–65. The writings of Jomo Kenyatta from *Facing Mount Kenya* (1938) to *Suffering without Bitterness* (1968) also indicate an intellect of stature. Oginga Odinga's *Not Yet Uhuru* and Tom Mboya's *Freedom and After* indicate some of the problems in which men of religion can be of service. Nigerian material of a similar nature should include works by or about Dr. Nnamdi Azikiwe, Obafemi Awolowo, and Ahmadu Bello. The apologias for the Biafran conflict take a reader deep into one of the predicaments of modern Africa—C. Odumwegwu Ojukwu's *Biafra* (New York, 1969) is just one example.

L. V. Thomas: *Les idéologies négro-africaines* (Dakar, 1965) is a handy guide to the writings from former French Africa. St. Clair Drake's essay in ed. William Hanna's *Independent Black Africa* (Chicago, 1964) is a good place to start a study of "the African personality" concept, while ed. Albert Berrian and Richard Long: *Négritude, essays and studies* (Hampton, Va., 1967) includes writers like Ki-Zerbo and Senghor. The section on *African Philosophy and World View* in King's *Religions of Africa* (pp. 103 f. and

Alexis Kagamé on p. 105) and the footnotes in Mbiti's *Religions and Philosophy* provide a fairly exhaustive reading list. An idea of Julius Nyerere's thought may be gained from a study of his speeches in *Uhuru na umoja, Freedom and Unity* (Nairobi, 1967) and *Uhuru na Ujamma, Freedom and Society* (1968). "Society" is a poor equivalent; "togetherness" in a group is indicated. The Arusha Declaration and the accompanying nationwide discussion is also important. It is to be hoped that more of Kenneth Kaunda's work will become available. At the moment his *A Humanist in Africa* (Nashville, 1966) and *Zambia Shall Be Free* (New York, 1963) are the only ones readily obtainable. A good epitome of African Christian thought, typical of similar statements from, for instance, Ghana in 1957 or Uganda in 1962 (the Uganda statement is notable for being jointly Catholic and Protestant), is contained in Christian Council of Nigeria: *Christian Responsibility in an Independent Nigeria* (Lagos, 1962) and the Catholic Bishops of Nigeria: *The Catholic Church in an Independent Nigeria* (Lagos, 1960).

Religion, politics and nationalism. Thomas Hodgkin: *Nationalism in Colonial Africa* (London, 1956, New York, 1957) remains basic. For a brief introduction to the topic since about 1955, see Immanuel Wallerstein's *Africa, the Politics of Independence* (New York, 1961) and *Africa the Politics of Unity* (New York, 1967). Gabriel A. Almond and James S. Coleman: *The Politics of Developing Areas* (Princeton, 1960) and James S. Coleman and Carl G. Rosberg: *Political Parties and National Integration in Tropical Africa* (Berkeley, 1964) go deeper. For even more intensive study the names to look up include Gwendolen Carter, Aristide Zolberg, and William Tordoff. Numerous useful essays and chapters which are not entirely taking in each other's washing will be found in collective works, for instance, David E. Apter: *Political Religion in the New Nations* in ed. Clifford Geertz: *Old Societies and New States* (Glencoe, 1963), and C. F. Adrian: "The Ideologies of African Leaders" in ed. David E. Apter: *Ideology and Discontent* (London and Glencoe, 1964).

On religion and politics at grass-roots level in those areas of Africa which their scholarship has preempted, see essays by Victor Turner, Monica Wilson, and Abner Cohen in ed. Marc Swartz: *Local-level Politics* (Chicago, 1969). On the Christian side—it is a pity that J. V. Taylor's African Penguin: *Christianity and Politics in Africa* (1957) has not been followed up, though D. A. Lowe's and Fred Welbourn's studies (mentioned below under Uganda) go into detail with Buganda. Victor D. Du Bois: "New States and an old Church" in Kalman H. Silvert's *Churches and States, the Religious Institution and Modernisation* (New York, 1967) is a valuable study, going into detail with the cases of Guinea, Congo-Brazzaville, and Ivory Coast. Probably again the books, autobiographies, and speeches of African political leaders of Christian background teach us best. Ndabaningi Sithole's *African Nationalism,* second edition (Oxford, Nairobi, and New York, 1968) is brilliant for this. (The first edition, written in 1957 and published at Cape Town in 1959, is worth reading in its own right.)

On *the Muslim side* Ali Mazrui of Mombasa and Makerere is the outstanding thinker who writes at amazing speed and publishes at regular intervals. See various essays in his *On Heroes and Uhuru-Worship* (London and New York, 1967) and *Towards a Pax Africana* (London and Chicago, 1967), and his (ed. with Robert I. Rotberg) *Protest and Power in Black Africa* (Oxford and New York, 1970).

Ibrahim Abu-Lughod: "The Islamic Factor in African Politics," *Orbis* VIII, 2 (summer, 1964), pp. 425-444 gives a most serviceable setting forth of the topic and the facts. On the East African side see W. Montgomery Watt: "The political relevance of Islam in East Africa," *International Affairs* XLII (1966), pp. 35-44. A great deal of material is to be found in collections of essays, for instance, Harry Heintzen: "The Role of Islam in the Era of Nationalism" in ed. W. H. Lewis: *New Forces in Africa* (Washington, 1962), and Vernon McKay: "The Impact of Islam on Relations among the New African States" in ed. J. H. Proctor: *Islam and International Relations* (New York, 1965). A book by Thomas Hodgkin on Islam in African politics is greatly to be desired. At the moment that veteran's thought must be hunted out. A *Festschrift* on his sixtieth birthday is forthcoming. From September through November, 1956 some nine articles by him appeared in *West Africa* on "Islam and Politics in West Africa." His "Islam and National Movements in West Africa" appeared in the *Journal of African History* III, 2 (1963), pp. 323-327 and "Islam History and Politics" in *Modern African Studies* I, 1 (1963), pp. 91–97. On the Arab role in Africa see Jacques Baulin's book of that title (Baltimore, 1962).

The dialogue between Christianity and Islam in Africa. The illustrated manuscript which shows Jesus and Muhammad conversing is from a copy of Rashid al-Din: *Universal History* made early in the fourteenth century which is in the University Library at Edinburgh, Scotland.

A detailed bibliography will be found in Kasozi and King's forthcoming *Islam and the Confluence of Religions in Uganda.* To put the matter briefly: on the Muslim side there is a fair amount to be found in print in the form of articles, pamphlets, and small books by regional Muslim leaders like Sheikh Shuaib of Uganda in such languages as Luganda, or in Swahili by Sheikhs al-Amin ibn Ali and Abdulla Saleh Farsy (the latter's *Tafsiri ya Kurani* was appearing in *fasciculi,* but it has proved impossible to obtain the last few issues in the U.S.A.).

Small works by Ahmadiyya writers refuting Christianity, in English, Twi,

Yoruba, Swahili, and Luganda, have been seen by the writer. Sometimes they are translations from the Urdu, but the tenor of them can be gauged from the notes on the Ahmadiyya Qur'an (English, Rabwah, Pakistan, 1955, reedited and reprinted, German, French, etc., Swahili, and portions in Luganda).

It has been possible to collect a great amount of oral material in such places as Dakar (Senegal); Accra, Kumasi, Wa, Sandema, Tamale (Ghana); Lomé (Togo); Lagos, Abeokuta, Ibadan, Kano (Nigeria); Eldoret, Kisumu, Nairobi, Mombasa (Kenya); Zanzibar, Tanga, Dar-es-Salaam, Tabora, Mwanza, Arusha, Muhoro in Tanzania; Kampala, Bombo, Masaka, Mbarara, Kabale, Jinja, Mbale, Hoima, Gulu and Arua in Uganda. In each of these towns it was possible to make it known that a visiting student of religion wanted to learn about Islam in that place and to request learned men to call and allow themselves to be visited. There was a generous readiness to extend hospitality and friendship. The material given is largely based on these meetings.

On the Christian side again the best material is at the oral level; there is, however, a fair amount in print which one can seek out. Since its inception after the great missionary conference at Edinburgh in 1910, *The Muslim World* has carried articles relevant to this subject. Its current editor, Willem Bijlefeld, is himself deeply versed in it. J. Spencer Trimingham has published pamphlets on this topic as a by-product of his major publications. Essays, monographs, and conference reports representative of each major period back to the 1890's can be dug out. For instance, for the 1950's see George Carpenter: "The Role of Christianity and Islam in Contemporary Africa" in ed. Charles Haines: *Africa Today* (Baltimore, 1955); A. Bernander: *The Rising Tide* (Rock Island, Ill., 1957 [being a translation from the Swedish]); and a report by Tracy Strong entitled *A Pilgrimage into the World of Islam,* World Alliance of Y.M.C.A.'s, Geneva (no date [1959?]). James T. Addison: *The Christian Approach to the Moslem* (New York, 1942; reprinted 1966) has a chapter with a useful bibliography on Islam in black Africa. R. Reusch's *Der Islam in Ost-Afrika* (Leipzig, 1930) unfortunately says more about Aden and Khartoum than Kampala and the lakes region. Maurice Delafosse, S. M. Zwemer, and W. R. Miller contributed a section on "Islam in Africa" to the 1926 Africa Special Number of *The International Review of Missions.* For earlier times see M. Klamroth: *Der Islam in Deutschostafrika* (Berlin, 1912), and A. P. Atterbury: *Islam in Africa, Its Effects, Religious, Ethical and Social* (New York, 1899).

Remarks, reports, and letters from missionaries in the field to their sending headquarters have still to be worked through and collated systematically. These vary from the bishop in East Africa early in this century who (not realizing that posterity might not allow him the virulent exaggeration privacy encourages) says of members of the other faith "most of them have V.D.," to the careful and in parts sympathetic report full of the desire to serve sent by Dr. W. Hutley in 1881 to the London Missionary Society from central Tanzania.

Some societies have given a good deal of attention to work among Muslims. Thus the Universities Mission to Central Africa encouraged Canon G. Dale in his work at Zanzibar and helped to publish his Swahili Qur'an (*Tafsiri ya kurani ya kiarabu,* London, 1923) and various books by him such as *Islam and Africa* (London, 1925) and *The Contrast between Christianity and Muhammadanism,* 9th ed. (London, 1948). Lyndon P. Harries followed this up for a while; see his *Islam in East Africa* (London, 1954). So also did Canon Robin Lamburn, who still lives among Muslims in the Rufiji delta (see his "Can Christians and Muslims work together?" *Dini na mila,* I, 4 (1966), pp. 21–29).

Despite this wealth of scattered written material the best account of how at last Christian and Muslim have begun to sit down together is still obtained by word of mouth. Pierre Benignus was killed in an air crash on Mount Cameroun; some of his writing is to be found at the Paris Mission headquarters and in obscure places like the old *Guide bleu* to French West Africa (A.O.F.), but his work continues at Ibadan at a Christian-Muslim Center named for him. John Crossley and James Ritchie have both sought to continue the dialogue with Islam. The doyen of it all is Franz Schildknecht, a White Father who has "sat among the people" in Algeria, West Africa, the Congo, and East Africa. His reports are not published. Following are some of his writings which are in print or published in mimeographed form: *Stoff zu theologischen Konferenzen ueber den Islam im Vergleich zu katholischer Theologie* (Ndanda, Tanzania, 1959); "Les musulmans et le Christianisme," *Parole et mission* (Paris, 1964), pp. 39–51; "l'Islam in Afrique orientale," in the same, pp. 571–580; "Der Islam in Ostafrika," *Die Katholischen Missionen* (Aachen, 1961); and a review in *Journal of Modern African Studies,* III, 1 (1965), pp. 147–151. His chapter on Islam in Tanzania in Kritzeck and Lewis: *Islam in Tropical Africa* (New York, 1969) is perhaps the most readily accessible piece of his work.

The religions and economic development. God has nothing against mammon till the latter aspires to be God. Religion plays an enormous role in development not only in slowing it up and in stabilization as it goes ahead. In the massive resettlement of people connected with the Akasombo Dam and Tema harbor in Ghana, it was vital that religious factors be taken into account, not only in providing the churches with sites in the new towns but in inviting the spirits of the old shrines to take up their abode elsewhere. In the development of trade in West Africa islamic commercial influence on the *dyula* was vital; the religious background of the Ismaili and other Asians in East Africa again assisted the development of that region. The evangelical

Christian emphasis on hard work, on the Bible *and* the plough, led to the expansion of the palm oil industry in east Ghana, cocoa growing in central Ghana, and cotton production in Yorubaland and Uganda. So far African economics had not produced its counterpart of Max Weber's *The Protestant Ethic and the Spirit of Capitalism* (translated Talcott Parsons; New York and London, 1930), nor Robert N. Bellah's *Tokugawa Religion* (Glencoe, Ill., 1957), nor Clifford Geertz' *Religion of Java* (Glencoe, 1960). Nor has any full-scale interpretative work on the part played by religion in African economics from the marxist side appeared. For a general understanding of some of the problems of development where men of religion can help, see George H. T. Kimble: *Tropical Africa, Problems and Promises* (New York, 1961); Reginald H. Green and Ann Seidman: *Unity or Poverty, the Economics of Pan-Africanism* (Penguin, 1968); Jagdish Bhagwati: *The Economics of Underdeveloped Countries* (London and New York, 1966), and René Dumont: *False Start in Africa* (French original 1962; English translation, London and New York, 1966).

Some regional and national bibliographies. West Africa. Fage's *History of West Africa* and Oliver and Atmore: *Africa since 1800* give most adequate advice on reading which can be supplemented from the notes after each chapter in Michael Crowder's large *West Africa under Colonial Rule* (London and Evanston, 1968). The following are a few national bibliographies to bring out special features of anglophone West Africa where the writer's work lay.

Sierra Leone. The Sierra Leoneans have produced their own historians, theologians, and so on for some time. A student can have fun looking for books and articles by A. T. Porter (historian), Edward Fasholé-Luke (church historian), Davidson Nicol (doctor and educationalist), John and Rena Karefa-Smart, and Harry Sawyerr. Christopher Fyfe: *A History of Sierra Leone* (Oxford and New York, 1963), a large book mainly on the nineteenth century. Peter Kup: *The Story of Sierra Leone* (Cambridge, 1964), only sixty pages but excellent. R. T. Parsons: *Religion in an African Society* (London and New York, 1964). Harry Sawyerr and W. T. Harris: *The Springs of Mende Belief and Conduct* (Freetown, London, and New York, 1968). Novels by William Conton and his excellent textbooks for high schools: *West Africa in History,* Books 1 and 2 (London, new ed., 1965). The Ethnic Folkways Records has a disc devoted to Mende music which includes traditional music and singing, Muslim prayers, women chanting in honor of the prophet, the dance of a masquerade spirit now classed as a *shaitan,* together with Christmas celebrations.

Liberia. The U. S. Army *Handbook for Liberia,* drawn up by the American University (Washington, 1964) has a section on religion and exhaustive bibliographies, which will give a lead in.

Ghana holds the West African prize for books on its religion. Here are a few. F. L. Bartels: *The Roots of Ghana Methodism* (Cambridge, 1965). H. Debrunner: *A Church between Colonial Powers* (London, 1965)—on the Evangelical Church in Togo and eastern Ghana. (Compare the case of the Bukoba Church cited under East Africa.) H. Debrunner: *A History of Christianity in Ghana* (Accra, 1967). Robert T. Parsons: *The Churches and Ghana Society, 1918–1955* (Leiden, 1963). Helene Pfann: *A Short History of the Catholic Church in Ghana* (Cape Coast, 1965). Noel Smith: *Presbyterian Church of Ghana* (Accra, London, and New York, 1967). S. G. Williamson: *Akan Religion and Christian Faith* (Accra, London, and New York, 1967). R. M. Wiltgen: *Gold Coast Mission History, 1471–1880* (Techny, 1956). There is an extensive pamphlet literature by Ghanaian writers, for instance Christian Dovlo: *Africa Awakes* (Accra, 1952); The Christian Council: *The Church in the Town* (Accra, 1951); The State Council of Akim-Abuakwa: *A Memorandum presented to the Synod of the Presbyterian Church* [on Church-State relations] (Kibi, 1941). A full list of these will be found in Harris W. Mobley: *The Ghanaian's Image of the Missionary, 1897–1965* (Leiden, 1970). Novels and plays by Kwesi Armah, Effuah Sutherland, etc. A number of Ghanaian "classical" High Life records have religious themes.

Nigeria. J. F. A. Ajayi: *Christian Missions in Nigeria, 1841–1891* (London, 1965). E. A. Ayandele: *The Missionary Impact on Modern Nigeria* (London and New York, 1966). M. Marioghae and J. Ferguson: *Nigeria under the Cross* (London, 1965). The novels of Chinua Achebe and Amos Tutuola, the plays and poems of Wole Soyinka mentioned above. Poems in ed. Gerald Moore and Ulli Beier: *Modern Poetry in Africa* (Penguin, rev. ed., 1965). The booklet and pamphlet literature; the interesting correspondence in local newspapers are overwhelming in their exuberant vitality and inexhaustible volume. The notes and bibliography in J. B. Webster's *African Churches among the Yoruba* (Oxford and New York, 1964) are a good place to begin.

The Sudan. K. D. D. Henderson: *Sudan Republic* (London and New York, 1965); P. M. Holt: *The Mahdist State in the Sudan* (Oxford and New York, 1958) and *A Modern History of the Sudan* (London and New York, 1961); Richard Gray: *A History of the Southern Sudan, 1839-1889* (Oxford and New York, 1961); Muddathiir Abdel-Rahim: *Imperialism and Nationalism in the Sudan, 1899–1956* (Oxford and New York, 1969); Oliver Albino: *The Sudan, a Southern Viewpoint,* (London, 1970).

East Africa in general. People who enjoy telephone books are recommended to read *The Catholic Directory of Eastern Africa* (Tabora, 1965). Roland Oliver: *The Missionary Factor in East Africa* (London and New York, 1952, 2nd ed., 1965) is a classic. B. A. Ogot and J. A. Kieran: *Zamani, a Survey of East African History* (Nairobi, London, and New York, 1968) is a book of essays giving most valuable background material. G. Were and D. Wilson: *East Africa through a Thousand Years* (Nairobi, London, and Evanston, 2nd impression, 1969) is valuable to a much wider field than the teachers for whom it was intended. F. B. Welbourn: *East African Christian* (Oxford and Nairobi, 1965) is a remarkable achievement in that it gives both background and detail. Studies of particular churches are of value. See for instance Levinus K. Painter: *The Hill of Vision* (Nairobi, 1951), which tells the story of the East Africa Yearly Meeting of Friends. It is said this is the largest Quaker meeting in the world. S. Rweyemamu and T. Msambure: *The Glories of the Catholic Church in Tanganyika* (Rome, 1963) is by two young priests about their church. Carl J. Hellberg: *Missions on a Colonial Frontier West of Lake Victoria* (Uppsala, 1965) tells the story of the church at Bukoba which is now under African leadership, having survived the strange antics of the colonialists.

The most worked-over piece of Christianity in East Africa is *Buganda* which is the central part of *Uganda.* Anyone wishing to go into deep waters may like to start from there. The following are a selection—J. F. Faupel: *African Holocaust* (London, 1962). H. P. Gale: *Uganda and the Mill Hill Fathers* (London, 1959). Brian Langlands and G. Namirembe: *Studies in the Geography of Religion in Uganda* (Kampala, 1967). This is a new and fascinating part of Religious Studies. See also Hildegard Johnson: "The Location of Christian Missions in Africa," *Geographical Review,* LVII, 2 (1965), pp. 168–202. David A. Low: *Religion and Society in Buganda, 1875–1900* (Kampala, 1957). Anne Luck: *African Saint, the Life of Kivebulaya* (London, 1963). J. V. Taylor: *The Growth of the Church in Buganda* (London, 1958). F. B. Welbourn: *Religion and Politics in Uganda, 1952–1962* (Nairobi, London, and Evanston, 1966). On *Islam in Uganda* a full bibliography will appear in Kasozi and King: *Islam and the Confluence of Religions in Uganda* (forthcoming). At the end of last Ramadan, a Luganda disc entitled *Alahumadini* reached "the top of the pops" in Kampala. Whether the gray-bearded sheikhs will be glad that the basic tenets of Islam which appear in song on this disc will now be heard in the bars, it goes to show there is a religious tinge in the modern youth culture.

The Congo-Kinshasa. Ruth Slade: *King Leopold's Congo* (London and New York, 1962), Ruth Slade: *The Belgian Congo* (London and New York, 1962). R. Anstey: *King Leopold's Legacy* (London and New York, 1966). P. Ceulemans: *La question arabe et le Congo* (Brussels, 1959; reprinted New York, 1969). A. Abel: *Les musulmans noirs de Maniema* (Brussels, 1960). Crawford Young: *Politics in the Congo* (Princeton, 1965). Patrice Lumumba: *Congo My Country* (London and New York, 1962).

The Congo-Brazzaville. Efraim Anderson: *Churches at the grass-roots* (London, 1968) is important as a close study of Protestant work in this former French area. His *Messianic Popular Movements in the Lower Congo* (Uppsala, 1958) has proved itself prophetic.

South Central Africa. A. J. Wills: *An Introduction to Central African History* (2nd ed., Oxford, 1967). L. H. Gann: *A History of Northern Rhodesia to 1953* (London and New York, 1964). A. J. Hanna: *The Story of the Rhodesias and Nyasaland* (1960; 2nd ed., London and New York, 1965). Ed. Brian M. Fagan: *A Short History of Zambia* (Oxford and Nairobi, 1966). Roland Oliver: *Sir Harry Johnston and the Scramble for Africa* (London, 1957). Ed. T. O. Ranger: *Aspects of Central African History* (London, 1968). Robert I. Rotberg: *Christian Missions and the Creation of Northern Rhodesia* (Princeton, 1965). George Mwase: *Strike a Blow and Die,* ed. R. I. Rotberg (Cambridge, Mass., 1967). Ndabaningi Sithole: *African Nationalism* (1957; 2nd ed., Oxford and New York, 1970). His *Obed Mutezo, Mudzimu Christian Nationalist* is forthcoming. The African Studies Center at Leiden is publishing two studies by Marthinus Daneel— *The God of the Matopo Hills* and *Zionism and Faith Healing in Rhodesia* which show clearly the vigor with which A.T.R. survives in various forms.

On Portugal in Africa. J. Duffy: *Portuguese Africa* (Cambridge, Mass., 1959), is still the best available book. His Penguin *Portugal in Africa* (1962) is also helpful. John Marcum's *Revolution in Angola,* vol. I (Cambridge, Mass. 1969), with vol. II forthcoming, will bring the Angolan side of the story up to date.

South Africa. There is no one adequate general background book, though Pierre van den Berghe's *South Africa, a Study in Conflict* (Berkeley, 1967), with its excellent bibliography, is a good place to start. E. A. Walker's *A History of Southern Africa* (3rd ed., 1957) has been of service. B. A. Pauw's *Religion in a Tswana Chiefdom* (Oxford, 1960) is a detailed study of the meeting of old and new religions in a small area. On Christianity see W. E. Brown: *The Catholic Church in South Africa* (London and New York, 1960); J. du Plessis: *History of Christian Missions in South Africa* (London, 1911; recently reprinted at Cape Town and republished at Mystic, Conn.); G. B. A. Gerdener: *Recent Developments in the South African Mission Field* brings it up to date to 1958; H. Davies: *Great South African Christians* (Oxford, 1951) gives some fine biographies. David M. Patons's *Church and Race in South Africa* (London and Naperville, 1958) is unfortunately only a small book and only covers 1952–1957. Also see Edgar H. Brookes and Amry Vandenbosch: *The City of God and the City of Man in Africa* (Lexington, 1963). The plays and novels of Alan Paton have done much to bring the tragedy of this country before the world ever since the appearance of *Cry, the Beloved Country* in 1948. Peter Hinchliff: *The Church in South Africa* (London, 1968) has a full bibliography. On *Islam in South Africa* see an exhaustive bibliography by Ruth Hampson (Cape Town, 1964). *Awake!,* the journal of the Young Men's Muslim Association of South Africa, often carries deeply serious discussions of the problems facing young Muslims as well as remarks like "the old sheikhs

tell us good Muslims wear beards. What then are goats. . . ."
Some Periodicals to browse in:
  Africa (London), since 1928.
  African Ecclesiastical Review (Masaka, Uganda), since 1959.
  African Historical Studies (Boston), since 1967.
  African Music Roodepoort, vol. 1 (1954); vol. 3 (1964).
  American Anthropologist (Washington), since 1888.
  Bulletin of the Society for African Church History (Nsukka and Aberdeen), since 1963.
  Cahiers des religions africaines (Kinshasa, Congo), since 1967.
  Dini na mila (Kampala, Uganda), since 1965.
  Ethnomusicology (Middletown, Conn.), since 1953.
  Ghana Bulletin of Theology (Legon, Ghana), since 1957.
  International Review of Missions (London), since 1910.
  Journal of African History (London), since 1960.
  Journal of the Historical Society of Nigeria (Ibadan), since 1956.
  Journal of Modern African Studies (Dar-es-Salaam and Cambridge, England), since 1963.
  Journal of Religion in Africa (Leiden), since 1968.
  Muslim World (Hartford, Conn.), since 1911.
  Nigeria Magazine (Lagos, Nigeria), quarterly, reached number 100 in April, 1969.
  Odu (Ibadan), since 1955.
  Orita (Ibadan), since 1969.
  Presence Africaine (Paris), since 1947.
  Sierra Leone Bulletin of Religion (Fourah Bay), since 1959.
  Sudan Notes and Records (Khartoum), since 1918.
  Tarikh (London), since 1965.
  Tanzania Notes and Records (Dar-es-Salaam), since 1936.
  Transactions of the Historical Societies of Ghana (Achimota and Legon, Ghana), since 1953.
  Uganda Journal (Kampala, Uganda), since 1933.
Material relevant to our subject will be found in publications coming out of innumerable conferences, for example: ed. Lalage Bown and Michael Crowder: *Proceedings of the First International Congress of Africanists* (Evanston, 1962); *Colloque sur les religions, Abidjan, 1961* (Paris, 1962). The regular publications of centers of African Studies or social research such as those at Dakar (*Institut fondamental* [formerly francais] *d'Afrique noire,* Legon, Ibadan, Nsukka, Makerere, Lusaka, etc.) often carry matter of vital interest to the religions man. May the *sunsum* (personality-soul) of Africa be placated (made cool) by such a libation of words poured forth!

Index